Ready, Set, Sell!

Retail Identity
Shop Layout & Fixturing
Category Displays

A Retail Guide for Small Business Operators
Written By:
Natalie Tan

Retail Excellence Consulting Services
Retail Learning Group

To H

January 2009

All rights reserved. Retail Excellence Consulting . Natalie Tan
No part of this publication may be reproduced in any form, or by any means
without a prior written consent from the author.

TABLE OF CONTENTS

Introduction   4

Chapter 1

Finding Your Soul: Retail Image and ID   6

Sign Design Activity   16

Chapter 2

The Capture: Shop Layout & Fixturing   37

Layout Exercise   65

Layout Exercise Answer Key   71

Chapter 3

Stage the Happy Ending: Category Adjacency Plan & Displays   75

Adjacency Plan & Display Case Studies   80

Store Transformations   104

Last Words   110

INTRODUCTION

Some stores thrive, while very similar shops fail. Two businesses targeting the same market offer comparable prices and products, but the one that succeeds offers something extra. Let us explore the IT factor that gets customers buying in some stores, while browsing in others.

The problem has always fascinated me. Being an avid shopper, I wonder what inspires me to buy from one store and not another? Simply put, the "feeling" generated inside a selling space affects our propensity to purchase. READY, SET, SELL is written to help small businesses understand and capture that elusive IT factor.

That insight brings fascinating repercussions. Together we'll look closely at the ins and outs of sales. An inability to sell the IT factor is not always the store's merchandise's fault. Since predisposition to buy rests on environmental factors, success is all about learning.

Could it really be that simple? Thus began my intense interest in this subject. Of course, having to shop as part of my research didn't hurt.

My work within the retail industry allowed me to indulge in this hobby. I reveled in watching how people shop, how they walk in a certain selling space and how they behave. Sitting inside a shopping center outside a store became fun. First I count the number of passers-by and then those that enter. What made some go inside? Is it a glance at the store window or a look toward an entrance filled with appealing merchandise? Once inside, do these people buy? If so, what and how much?

Have you ever visited stores that fired up your shopping mood while others left you cold? Something in these stores drives us to buy or not. As an avid proponent of store atmospherics for many years, the power of an effectively merchandised store to bring in increased sales never ceases to amaze me. Appealing displays, well-lit focal points and enticing scents propel me to those spaces and pique my interest. However, what excites me are the "cold" stores where the power of an effective retail environment remains untapped. My mind races to examine possible layouts that will yield the highest customer penetration. My fingers itch to rearrange the merchandise presentation and visual displays to maximize both silent and active multiple selling.

My passion turned into a business helping small retailers. From food units to hardware tools, from lingerie shops to chiropractors' offices, my adventures in retail live on.

My goal for this book is to provide you, the retailer, with some tools to improve shop performance. If you are just setting up a new shop, I hope this series gives you an effective foundation to build your enterprise. The first chapter shows how retail image and identity, as well as the logo chosen bears a significant impact on how your business is first perceived. The shop layout and fixturing section provides you with case studies on how to create an effective selling space while the final chapter on display strategies gives you an idea of what to put where, why and how. At the end of each section is a series of short activity pages or case studies that enable you to apply techniques learned.

FINDING YOUR SOUL:
Retail Image and Identity

Does your store have a personality?

What do you mean, you ask? I mean, who are you? What are you selling? Who are you selling to?

Why should people shop at your store?

What's in it for them?

Ask people what they sell, and get a product reply: shoes, clothing, home accessories, etc. What I'm looking for is what they're really selling. Depending on specific categories, a shoe store can sell comfort and health while another can sell fashion and social acceptance. A woman's lingerie shop can sell romance, sex, health or casual fun depending on the type of merchandise they carry. Home accessories can sell an atmosphere of well-being or prestige. This is not to say that stores are limited to one selling idea, just that there is usually a dominant idea they become popular for.

Now, what do you sell?

Think about the people you want to sell to. Choose a segment of the market you can effectively communicate with. What does this group want to see? What do they want to feel as they shop? What do they aspire to own or become?

As kids we all played pretend games. Some boys aspire to become G.I. Joes, some wanted to be fire fighters, police officers, doctors, etc. My 4-year old niece wishes to be a princess when she grows up. As a loving aunt, I shower her with princess toys, outfits, accessories, books, etc. We visit places where her imagination can take off. For that one moment, she can feel like she is indeed Sleeping Beauty. What a wonderful world, this make-believe.

You can deliver an experience like this to your customers. If you were that customer walking into your store, what would your fantasy experience be like? Imagine the perfect storefront. What do you want to first see? What colour feeds your fantasy?

Think about smell. Sweet and fruity? Sensual and fleeting? Clean and clear?

Does it feel warm or cool? Are you walking on something soft or substantial? Do you hear music? What else?

Let me walk you around my fantasy cottage shop. It is just the beginning of the holiday season. The air is crisp outside but as I walk inside the shop, it is nice and warm. Not too warm, mind you, just warm enough that I am not too cold but can still wear my jacket comfortably. (My fantasy does not involve removing my bulky jacket and having to carry it while I shop.) I close my eyes at the beginning of this journey to heighten my senses. I feel the colour. It has the golden hues of the sun and the reddish tones of a fire. I hear soft background music, the rustle of other customers shopping and a child's voice happy over something discovered. Merry laughter comes from a corner somewhere. I hear the rustle of a paper bag being filled at the cash counter, and the sales associate thanks a customer with a smile (yes, I can hear a smile). Large planks of wooden floor boards creak as shoppers walk around. Oh, is that fresh pine I smell in the air? Some pine, but also the smell of hot sweet cider. Smells like a loving home! The aromas are not too strong, just so that I can smell it coming from one direction more than others.

Now I slowly open my eyes. This is what a slice of heaven must look like. The walls are made of wood that has wonderfully aged. The fixtures show some wear but are lovingly cared for. There are places where the wood has already smoothed after years of customers touching the same spots. A riot of colours surrounds. I can see happiness and love all around.

What am I selling? Love, of course, to family and special friends. Tradition, too. This is a place where gifts are meaningful and passed on from one generation to the next.

Now it is your turn. Walk me through your world. Describe what you want your customers to feel, hear, smell, touch and see. What special touches will you leave for customers to find? See how much of your store is part of you? After all, it is your shop. Don't let someone else's opinion cloud your judgment. This is your vision, your character. Every time a customer walks in, share with them a part of you!

The Christening

When a core identity has been established, begin working on a name. Let's use the holiday cottage store as an example. You know how it looks and feel. What name would you christen it? Wings of Love? Yuck, nothing too flighty please. Imagine a Wings of Love store? I see it as being pink with lots of feathers. Definitely not the homelike cottage-feel. How about Natalie's Cottage? No, while it is great to see my name in big bold letters, somehow, Natalie does not really evoke the cottage feel. How about Grandpa's Attic? It's not romantic, but it's very "cocooning"; a place Mom can bring the kids and spend hours discovering treasures. It has a feel of a time that is comforting and safe. These are the feelings I would like to promote.

If I said the cottage has the feel of a new beach cottage and you can smell the ocean, the name could be something like "Sirens" especially if this store is geared to carrying women's fashions and gifts. If the cottage is in a mountain resort, it could be "The Log Cabin". Imagine how each name is written and the colours used. Sirens might look like this-

SIRENS

where the letters evokes an almost aquatic feel. The colour needs to be strong because Sirens evoke feminine images of strength.

The Log Cabin on the other hand seems like a given. One can almost envision lettering made of wood logs. If it is a popular price point,-

THE LOG CABIN

wood brown seems appropriate. However, if the store targets affluent customers, then it may look like this,-

The Log Cabin

The Chalet

maybe even calling it a Chalet. If the specialty is kids, then Log Cabin in bright colours is effective.

LOG CABIN

Dress for Work

Store name, along with design, must support the image you are selling to customers. For example, a white shirt can be sold for $10 at a "Dress for Work" retail cart while the same white shirt can be sold for $50 or more at a shop named "MODA ITALIA". Of course the Moda Italia shop may have black lacquer fixtures, rich carpeting and the smell of success in the air. This is not to say that the Dress for Work shirt will make you any less successful, just that when you need more confidence during a presentation, you will likely wear the Italia Moda shirt for added support. Store image and identity lends itself to circumstances that customers turn to when they need the very thing a store promotes.

MODA ITALIA

What Colours Should Be Used?

How Big Should Fonts Be?

One of the things I notice in some logos is lack of consideration for the intended market. What I mean is, size, colour and design do not match the message. A high-end pen shop I once saw used all capital letters in a logo that looks like this—

HIGH END PEN SHOP

The large font and colourful lettering made the shop's target market to be children, rather than affluent successful businesspeople intended. Would you really want to spend $1000 on a pen at this store? It would be more effective to convey success and prestige using a font that evokes images of strength and foundation. Something like -

High End Pen Shop

If the target is successful young entrepreneurs, then a modern and clean font in silver gray is effective.

HIGH END PEN SHOP

Read the logos in a voice matching the design. Can you almost hear the voice reading each logo aloud? The first one would sound funny, the middle one haughty and the last one deep and dignified.

SIGN DESIGN: FONT EXERCISE 1

SIZE

How does size affect perceived target market and business identity?
Which one the following best represents the following characteristics?

Popular Price Point; Appeals to a wide market
Mid-price Point; Narrower segregated target market
High Price Point; Exclusive market

Day Spa

Day Spa

Day Spa

Day Spa

Day Spa

Day Spa

Answer Key:
Popular Price Point: Large Plain Font (Upper Right Column)
Mid-price Point: Medium Sized Casual Font (Middle Left Column)
High Price Point: Smaller Stylized Font (Lower Right Column)

Colours are powerful tools in driving certain atmosphere or moods. Primary colours appeal to the broadest range of the market, along with orange and green. Different tones can be used to appeal to a smaller segment. A popular priced children's store may go for the bright fun colours while the higher end ones will use more muted versions. A teens store selling fashions may use fuchsia and turquoise expressing energy (bottom left pair) while the same store aiming for higher price points may go for muted tones of the same colour. (Bottom right pair)

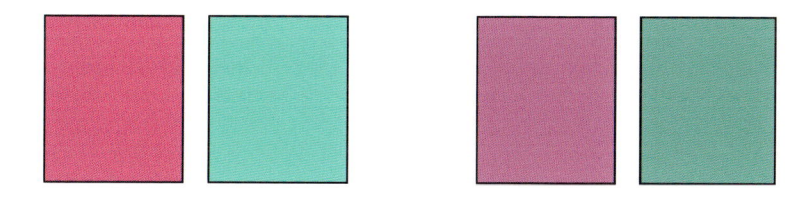

There are several good books on colours and what they mean. Learning about colour will provide guidelines for establishing your own identity.

SIGN DESIGN: FONT EXERCISE 2

COLOUR

How does colour affect perceived target market and business identity?
Choose which colours you think represent the following specific characteristics:

Soothing & Refreshing
Warm & Friendly
Va-vavoom & High Energy
Clean & Medical

Day Spa   *Day Spa*

Day Spa   *Day Spa*

Answer Key:
Soothing & Refreshing: Green
Warm & Friendly: Orange
Va-vavoom & High Energy: Red
Clean & Medical: Blue

SIGN DESIGN: FONT EXERCISE 3

Below is a list of logos using the same store name but shown in differing fonts. Match which ones identify with the product line listed on the right.

aerine   Antique Furniture

Aerine   Electronic Gadgets

Aerine   Girls' Dresses

Aerine   Children's Toys

Aerine   Modern Home Accessories

Aerine   High-end Ladies' Fashions

Answer Key: 1. Modern Home Accessories; 2. Girl's Dresses; 3. Electronic Gadgets; 4. Antique Furniture; 5. Children's Toys; 6. High-end Ladies Fashions

19

SIGN DESIGN: FONT EXERCISE 4

PUTTING IT ALL TOGETHER

Lets now combine all 3 elements. How do colour, font style and size affect customer perception of target market and image? Take a look at the sample table below. Is this a good model for logos? Are the 3 elements congruent to the projected image? Whenever there is incongruence in any of these, confusion results.

When customers have difficulty understanding what you stand for, they are less likely to enter your premises.

Day Spa

Day Spa

Day Spa

PUTTING IT ALL TOGETHER

What is incongruent? Should the highly stylized font at the bottom of the page be in red? What about the middle logo? Is orange a good colour for this? Is the size appropriate for the Times New Roman font of the first logo? Is green the best colour for this?

Answer Key:
Better font size and colours for each logo is shown below.

Day Spa

Day Spa

Day Spa

Customers Need To Understand What A Shop Is About Before Entering

Communication is established prior to a customer entering the store. Exterior signs, store displays and entrance size have a bearing on how a store can effectively send the message across. While we've discussed how store name, and exterior sign can affect this, those need to be supported by everything else the customer sees.

Exterior design can affect how a store is perceived. Going back to the cottage shop example, can you envision what the architecture should look like? Certainly not shiny stainless aluminum! How about large French windows with a wooden façade that's shabby chic?

Think about entrance size? Should the store be wide open with no doors or should it be a single wooden door held open, maybe with a dried floral wreath hanging? The size of a store's entrance can send varying messages of price points. A large wide entrance can mean that the store is for everyone, with popular price points. Mid-sized entrances can be a little bit more discriminating almost saying price points are attainable, but not entirely popular. Smaller entrances, similar to those seen on exclusive jewellery shops or prestige designers stores, communicate that the shop may not be suited to everyone's tastes. Rather, they are appealing to a smaller, more concentrated segment of the market.

Let the Selling Begin

Signs are a great way to communicate to customers. Better yet, signs assists in selling. According to Paco Underhill, author of the bestseller Why We Buy, hierarchies exist in sign viewing. For example, when we visit food units, we all tend to look up to the menu board. This is about 6 – 8' high. Our sight then moves to just above the cash register when we interact with the sales associate. At this point, we find signs that suggest upsizing orders or adding menu items. As we pick our food tray up and go to the condiment stand, there might be a sign suggesting dessert. Then when we sit, a table tent card suggests additional items or reminds us of any store promotions. When eating alone, many people read to reduce awkwardness. This also signals the desire for privacy and deters interruptions from strangers. If you are like me, I tend to read everything I can. This includes the trademark registry on the tray liners. At each stage of this process, the operator is given an opportunity to layer their message and at the same time, capitalize on a captive audience.

Inside stores, our ceiling may not go as high as 12'. This section is usually reserved for directional signs similar to ones we see in shopping malls. They indicate location of exits, elevators, food courts, and washrooms among others.

What concerns most shop owners are the ones they should show, from 6 – 9' high. This is a good location for category or department signs. Use these as needed. Product presentation alone can effectively convey product categories and large promotional messages.

Anything below 6' is a good area for more targeted signs. For example, Item signs, Product line signs, Price signs, Product Information signs and medium to small sized Promotional signs

SIGNS MAKE SHOPPING EASY

The importance of signs in the store cannot be emphasized enough. Signs allow customers to identity store organization, thereby making it easy to shop. Signs specify what merchandise customers can expect to find in a selling unit. When advertised specials are signed. It cuts the wasted time customers might take to look for them. It allows more time for browsing other products. Sale items and those on Special Promotions benefit by directing customers to their location. When viewed from outside the store these signs can propel customers into the shop. New Arrival signs provide shoppers a reason to visit.

Log Bedroom Suite

Expertly hand-made by local artisan Joe Smith, this environmentally friendly log suite utilizes reclaimed underwater logs. Strong maple logs produce the best texture, colours and scent!

QUEEN SIZE LOG BED $ XXX
LOG NIGHTSTAND $ XXX
LOG ARMOIRE $ XXX

Heavenly Outhouse

When price signs contain product information, such as features and benefits they become part of a silent selling strategy. When they feature promotions for coordinating items they also utilize multiple selling opportunities. Product information reminds customers why they need the product and reassures them of their buying decision.

25

SIGNS SELL FOR YOU

According to Sonja Larson, author of Signs That Sell, an item that is labelled can increase sales up to 24% over items with no signs. When features and benefits are included, sales can even increase up to 49%.

Eighty percent of customers shop without a list and 53% make unplanned purchases. You want these shoppers to buy their unplanned purchase at your store. LEK Partnership came out with the study "Sales Impact of Signs". It maintains that in one of their experiments, in-store displays and signs led to sales increases of up to 355%.

Sales are higher on signs that list product features or benefits.

Data from Sonja Larson and LEK Partnership derived from:
Sonja Larson, Signs That Sell, Published by Insignia Systems Inc. 1991

MACHINE PRINT vs. HAND WRITTEN SIGNS

Signs are an extension of your image and ID. For the most part, signs work to establish product credibility. This is especially evident in food units. Would you buy a burger and fries from an establishment whose signs are hand-written in a felt pen or cardboard? What does it say about food quality, store operations and owner credibility? This is not to say that hand-written signs have no place in retailing. Market bazaars and lemonade stands where one wishes to promote very low prices or convey down home 'charm' may well benefit from this. Needless to say, the signs still need to maintain certain standards in legibility, cleanliness and neatness.

LEK Partnership's study maintains that sales can increase up to 49% when signs were changed from hand-written to machine print.

Not many would be tempted to pay $230 for a vase with a hand-written sign such as the one shown above. Instead of enhancing product values these signs surely de-value them. Besides this valuable item needs a conversational sign telling customers why it deserves the asking price.

SIGN CLASSIFICATIONS

The two basic sign classifications are operational signs and selling signs. Operational signs deal with store policies such as returns and exchanges. They include food and beverage policies, as well as change room guidelines. Operational signs also outline store hours, phone numbers and at times contain directional information

Examples of Operational Signs Below:

Returns & Exchanges

Returns are Accepted on Unworn Items Purchased
Within 7 Days with Tags Attached
Exchanges are Accepted on Damaged Items Only
Within 7 Days with Receipt

THANK YOU

Forever Yours Lingerie

Store Hours

Monday	10 am - 5 pm
Tuesday	10 am - 5 pm
Wednesday	10 am - 5 pm
Thursday	10 am - 5 pm
Friday	10 am - 8 pm
Saturday	10 am - 5 pm
Sunday	11 am - 4 pm

Selling signs refer to price signs, promotional and sale signs, shelf talkers, etc. all of which are shown below.

CATEGORY SIGN

Forever Yours Lingerie — **New Arrivals**

Forever Yours Lingerie — **Body Shapers**

ITEM/PRICE SIGN

Rose Lace Nightset
$189
Forever Yours Lingerie

PRICE with FEATURE/BENEFITS

Rose Lace Nightset
- 3 Piece Set: Bra, Panty & Robe
- Delicate Venetian Lace
- Super Soft Jacquard Silk

$189
Forever Yours Lingerie

MULTIPLE SELLING SIGNS

Fantasie

Stay Dry Sports Set	$139
INDIVIDUAL PRICES:	
Stay-Dry Sports Bra	$89
Stay-Dry Briefs	$29
Stay-Dry Shorts	$39

Forever Yours Lingerie

SALE

Shaper Briefs
2 / $48

REGULAR PRICE $29 each

PROMOTIONAL & SALE SIGNS

SALE
End of Season Clearance
Upto **70% off**

CONVERSATIONAL SIGNS

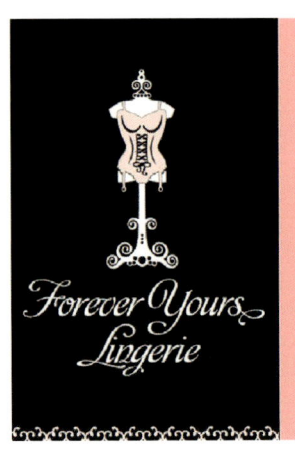

Venetian Lace Trim Robes

Direct from Italy, these Venetian Lace Trimmed Robes are embellished with delicate hand-made rose lace. Expertly crafted by the Rochas Company, these robes are the ultimate in luxury. Lightweight and feathery soft silk caress your skin with every move. Designed by Madame Rochas herself, this exquisitely cut robe skims your figure and offers a sensual glimpse of skin.

Forever Yours Lingerie

SEASONAL SIGNS

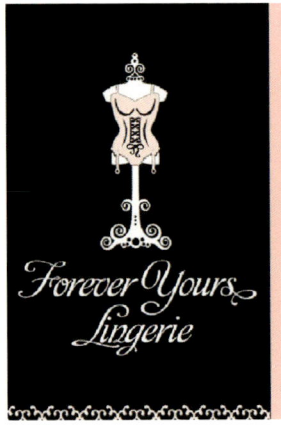

Holiday Print Robes
$29

ITEM PRICE TAG

"Natalie put together a signage plan for us which is not only beautiful but consistent. I am sure the consistency of the signage throughout our new store will help clients find what they need quickly and easily."

Sonya Larson, Owner, Forever Yours Lingerie, Langley, BC, Canada

LAYERING YOUR MESSAGE

Signs come in a variety of sizes. The most common seen in shops are poster size, about 22x28; medium ones at 8.5x11 or 5.5x7 for unit toppers. Small shelf talkers vary from 3.5x5; 2.5x3 or even 3.5'x 3", to line an entire shelving unit.

Sign design principles are not limited to shops but are also applicable to food units. The examples below show how sign hierarchy can be applied.

Below: Cle Elum Bakery achieves layering from menu boards to unit toppers and price item signs.

A Conversational Sign informs customers of the value received whenever they purchase from your shop. From single items to shop history, conversational signs are a great way to converse with customers.

CATEGORY SIGN

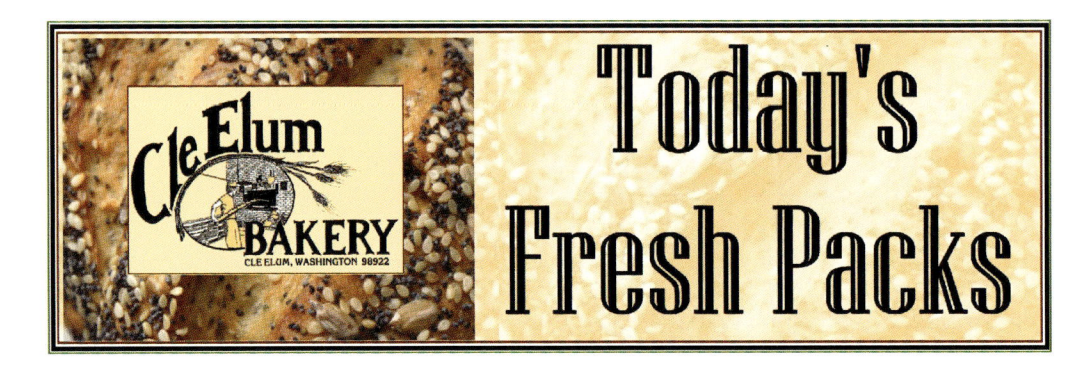

Today's Fresh Packs
Cle Elum BAKERY

ITEM/PRICE SIGN

Today's Fresh Packs
Assorted Bags
$8.99
Tradition & Quality You Can Trust

PRICE with FEATURE/BENEFIT

Try Our Most Popular Bread
DUTCH CRUNCH
Savory French Bread Topped With Rice Flour
Introduces A Whole New Bread Experience
$2.95
Tradition & Quality You Can Trust

MULTIPLE SELLING SIGNS

Freshly Baked Cookies
Singles $.40
Dozen $4.00
Tradition & Quality You Can Trust

SIGN FOR ADJACENT CAFÉ SHOP

THE BAKERY HOUSE
COMBO
HOLIDAY TURKEY
DELIGHT
+ 1 BAG OF CHIPS + POP
$7.50

BUSINESS CARD/LOYALTY CARD

Cle Elum BAKERY
Original Brick Oven In Use Since 1906

Ivan & Claudia Osmonovich
501 East First Street
Cle Elum, Washington 98922
509.674.2233

THE BAKERY HOUSE
509.674.6746

donut1@cleelum.com

SEASONAL SIGN

Pumpkin Pie
$9.95
Tradition & Quality You Can Trust

32

Food Unit Sign Layering: Banner Sign, Menu Boards, Posters, Category Signs, Price Item Signs, Table Toppers & Business Loyalty Cards

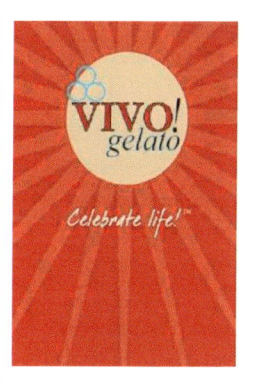

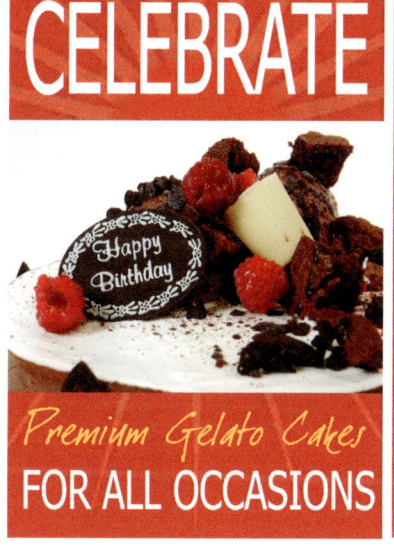

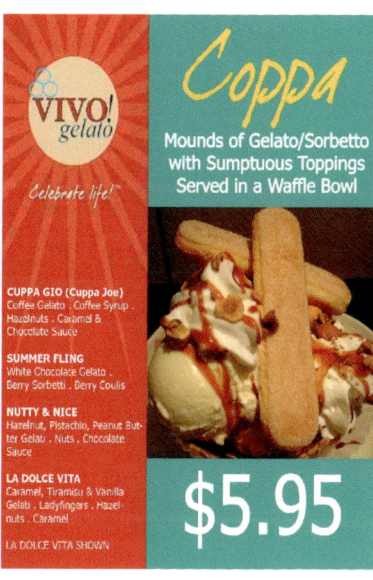

SIGN DESIGN

Understanding where the optical center of a sign is, provides retailers with a guide on how to convey effective messages. It is vital to consider the space, as well as the message sequence. The simplest way to determine placement is to draw an X mark on the sign sheet. Right above the intersection of the X, can be marked with a circle. This circle represents the optical center of the sign. Ensure that this space occupies a vital message.

TONE OF SIGNS

The message's tone is as important as the information you wish to convey. Keep them positive, and establish good customer rapport. For example, instead of saying DO NOT OPEN PACKAGES, a positive tone is THANK YOU FOR REFRAINING FROM OPENING PACKAGES. THIS ENSURES THAT OUR PRICES REMAIN LOW.

In the example below, instead of "IF YOU REQUIRE ANYTHING FROM THIS CABINET, PLEASE ASK AN ASSISTANT", why not write "WE WILL BE HAPPY TO SHOW THESE WATCHES TO YOU". Why tell customers to ask for an assistant IF they require anything, when in reality, who really requires anything?

THE CAPTURE:
Shop Layout & Fixturing

The Capture: Ready, Set, Go

Your shop has a magnificent storefront. Its windows are captivating. Customers stop to look at them and want to step inside.

Go! Go... I say!

Where do they venture? Do shoppers walk straight to a feature table? A smart shop owner arranges merchandise to reflect how they wish customers to shop. Do you want them to encircle the entire selling area? Maybe veer to the left? Some shops are best off organized like a grocery store. Other work well directing customers close to the walls.

Careful design considerations must begin with the customers' entry. Follow with a plan that determines how they will move through your selling area. The better the flow, the more areas buyers go to, the more merchandise is seen, and the higher the probability of sales. This is not a new idea. Yet, it never ceases to amaze me how retailers lose sight of the flow factor, agonizing more over wall colour than store layout.

Give some thought to how you want customers to shop your merchandise. This is more than just placing the cash desk upfront to monitor shoplifters. It goes further than the secondary consideration; floor fixtures. Setting up effective shopping patterns involves careful study of the direction of the majority of traffic, and serious contemplation to how walls and columns affect space. The goal is to create four key scenarios. Present an easy entry point. Then set up an unobstructed path to promote browsing. Work to provide areas that will create merchandise stories. Always ensure easy access to products and their eventual purchase.

Begin with the End

How does one begin? Working with small retailers, my goal is to keep projects as simple as possible, with the least amount of expense. If the budget allows for a store designer, this is great! However, for the most part, this is a luxury only few can afford. Either way, I encourage you to start from the end.

Take a serious look at the products. Most people start with layout by determining the preferred location of the cash desk. Preferred by the owner is not necessarily the most convenient space for customers, by the way. Store owners tend to choose a cash desk location that affords the best view of potential thieves, while at the same time avoids spatial impediments such as columns. I, on the other hand, begin by looking at the products. Keep them in mind and consider the following:

1. Types of merchandise categories; gives an idea as to how many sections to create
2. Volume of merchandise per category or number of sub-categories; determines optimal area allotted to each
3. Types of product per category; determines types of fixture and their dimensions

The next step is to reflect on wall locations and supporting columns. Build traffic paths or main aisles. Not all retailers are blessed with shops having no visible columns. For many, columns are design hassles looked upon with disdain; they block sightlines and make a space tight. At times, columns are unsightly. However, when faced with lemons, make lemonade. Make use of columns as area focal points, or make pillars disappear by building merchandisers around them.

TOP PHOTO: Before renovations, columns painted in white dominate the view.
MIDDLE: This diagram shows that painting columns black make them less visible.
PHOTO ABOVE: After renovations, the row of columns become less dominant.

Aisles bring people from one end of the store to the other. They allow customers to walk from one section to the next in smooth flow. Aisles play an important role in ensuring as many merchandise stories are viewed as possible. They allow customers access to products. If they can't see your goods, or touch them, they won't be buying.

Before going further, let's get more familiar with basic layouts. Understanding the fundamental possibilities provides retailers with guidelines in creating their own store structure.

GRID

We see Grids in grocery stores, drug stores, stationery, hardware, department stores and super-centres. They allow 'seeker' type customers the most organized and efficient way to shop. They are also ideal for off-price retail such as dollar stores or clothing warehouses.

The sample layout diagrams below and in the following pages show a typical 25' x 40' selling space.

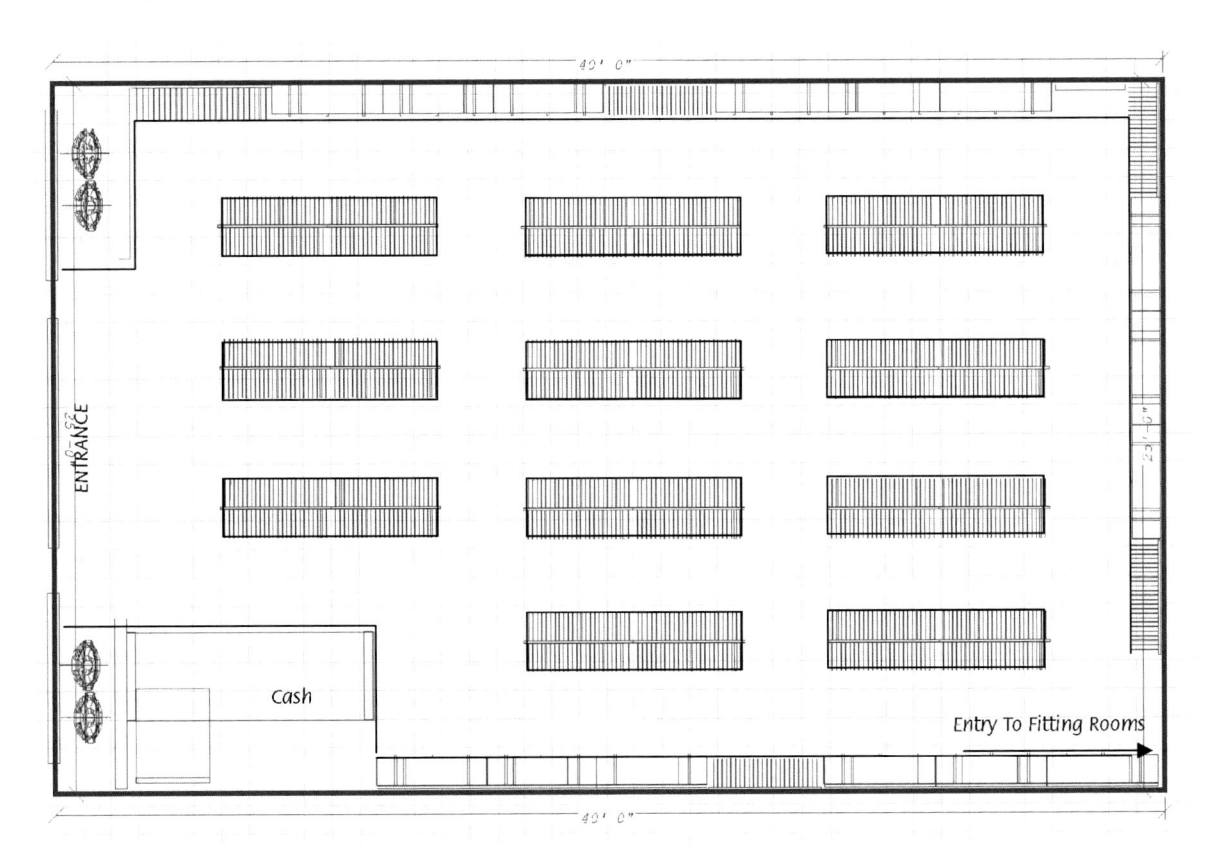

ABOVE: A sample grid layout designed for a discount clothing shop.

FREE-FLOW

For customers who love to browse, a Free-flow layout encourages wandering, revealing one surprise, after another. Aisles in this layout are determined by fixture placement, often in a balanced and logical sequence. Small boutiques and gift shops that carry exclusive merchandise benefit from Free-flow structure.

With apologies for the generalization, I have to say that Free-flow layouts baffle a good number of men. Case in point, my husband won't even bother entering a store without a straight main aisle. Males are most commonly classified as seekers; those shoppers who want a clear indication of where they're going to achieve their objectives. There isn't room for fuzziness. For him, a Radio Shack (now called The Source) is a perfect store, while La Senza, a lingerie boutique, is the equivalent of a maze.

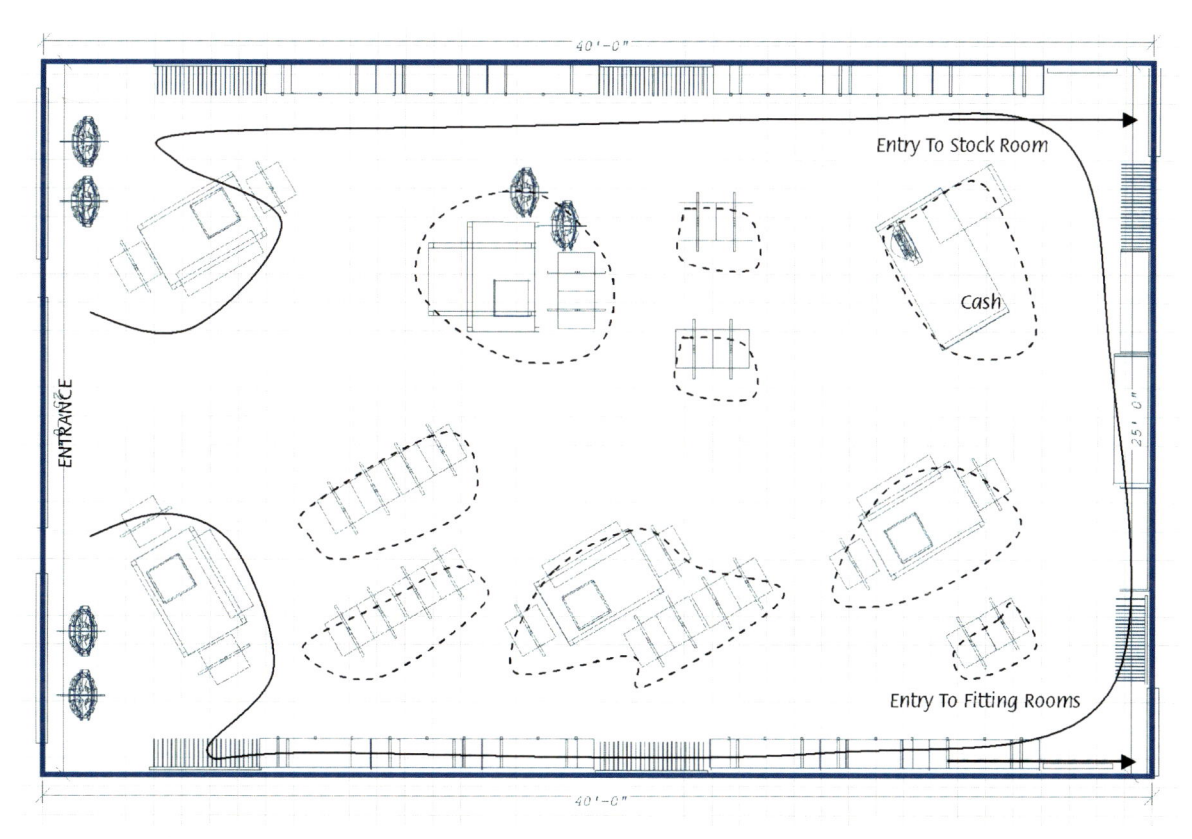

ABOVE: This free-flow layout may be used by a specialty clothing retailer.

SOFT-AISLE

When a majority of the merchandise is displayed on walls, getting customers to shop them is crucial. The Soft-aisle creates a main traffic path hugging the walls, thereby encouraging customers to spend time in these areas. Secondary aisles are then formed in the middle of the store, which allow for fixture groupings.

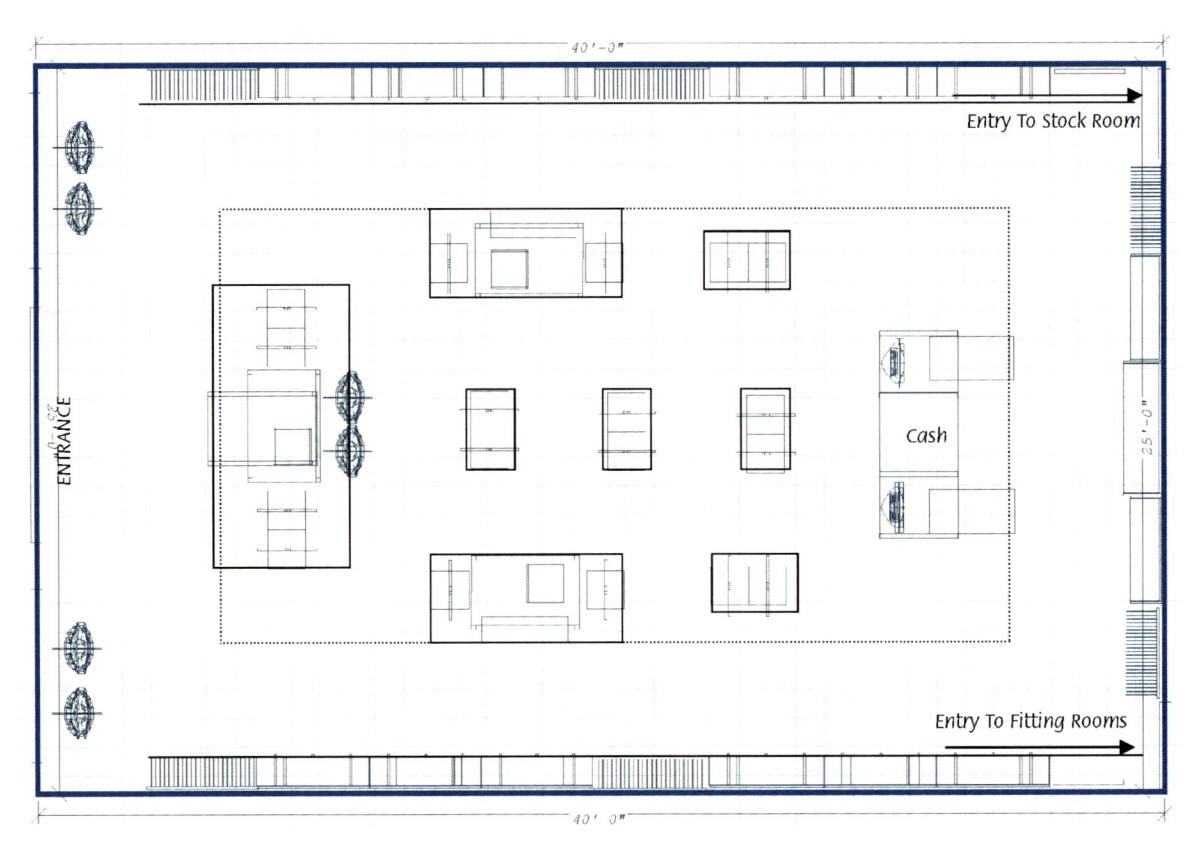

ABOVE: This soft-aisle clothing store shows an obvious main path that encourages customers to prioritize the walls.

MINIMAL

High-end prestige type stores often go for the Minimal layout. It is a plan type that provides customers with open areas to view products. When product intensity determines perceived product value, a Minimal layout will ensure enhanced product values. This layout is best left to prestige designer stores, unless you are selling $1000 items. Less affluent customers may be deterred from entering.

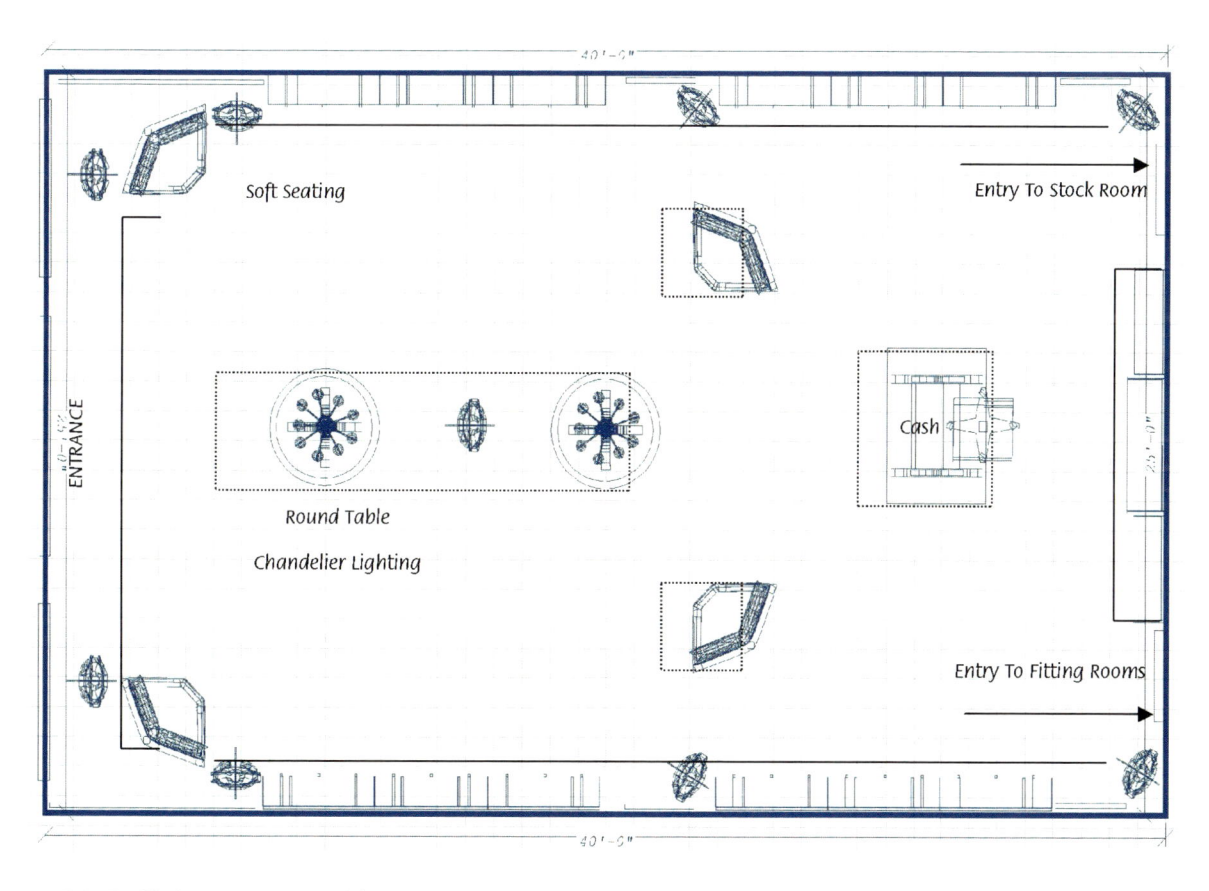

ABOVE: Clothing on a minimal layout is spread throughout the open space. While typical clothing stores will house one hanger per inch of hangrail, minimal shops may sport less clothing, usually one item per short straight arm unit. Majority of their merchandise may be faced-out in contrast to a high density combination side-out and face-out placements.

RACETRACK

The Racetrack allows customers to move around the store by giving them a 'track' that leads from entrance to rear and then back. The path encircles the entire floor area, allowing for the most merchandise to be seen. The Racetrack is a great layout for new retailers. It is easy to maintain and keep organized. By combining this with a Free-flow or a Grid, retailers have flexibility. The object of the game is to ensure that customers do not race through the Racetrack. This is where focal points and power walls play a crucial role in getting customers to stay longer in your store. (Discussed in the following pages.)

COMBINATION

As mentioned, the Racetrack layout can be combined with either a Free-flow or a Grid to allow for flexibility. Combining different layout types is not limiting. For example, a gift boutique may use Free-flow in the first half of the store while the back section features sale racks in Grid style.

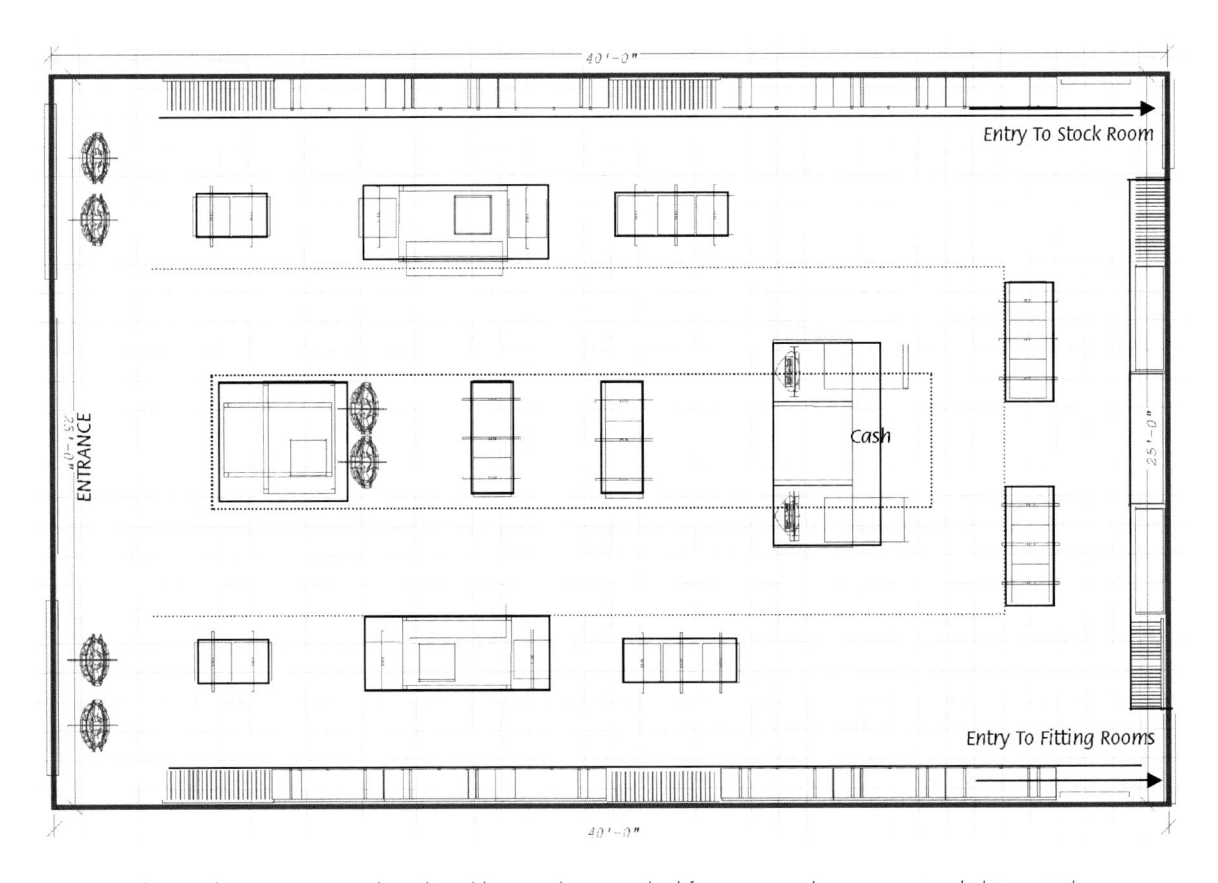

ABOVE: The combination racetrack and grid layout above is ideal for any popular price-point clothing retailer.

STEP 1: TRAFFIC PATH

Creating an effective layout begins with several possible studies. Using graph paper, allocate one square to equal a square foot of your store. Use the step-by-step guide below for assistance.

1. Draw the shop walls on the graph paper.

2. Plot out windows and entrances.

3. Determine the best location for a cash area. One of the best areas for a cash desk is center and mid-back, depending on store shape. Other probable choices include off to one side, against a wall, and either mid or back corner. Keep in mind it is best if the cash desk is not the first thing a customer sees.

4. Sketch 'bubbles' to represent the number of merchandise categories.

In your first attempt, try for a Racetrack layout, unless your shop is more suited to a Grid, such as a grocery, stationery or hardware store. Sample diagrams of a gourmet food shop follow next page.

The sample below shows a diagram of Academie du Gourmet of Embrun, Ontario. Their walls and entrances are plotted on graph paper. A racetrack layout is used to maximize flow from the main and secondary entrance towards the cooking school entrance at the back of the store. The cask desk is located in the centre mid-back section to encourage customer flow around it. Both the retail section and the cooking school may take advantage of the cash desk's convenient location.

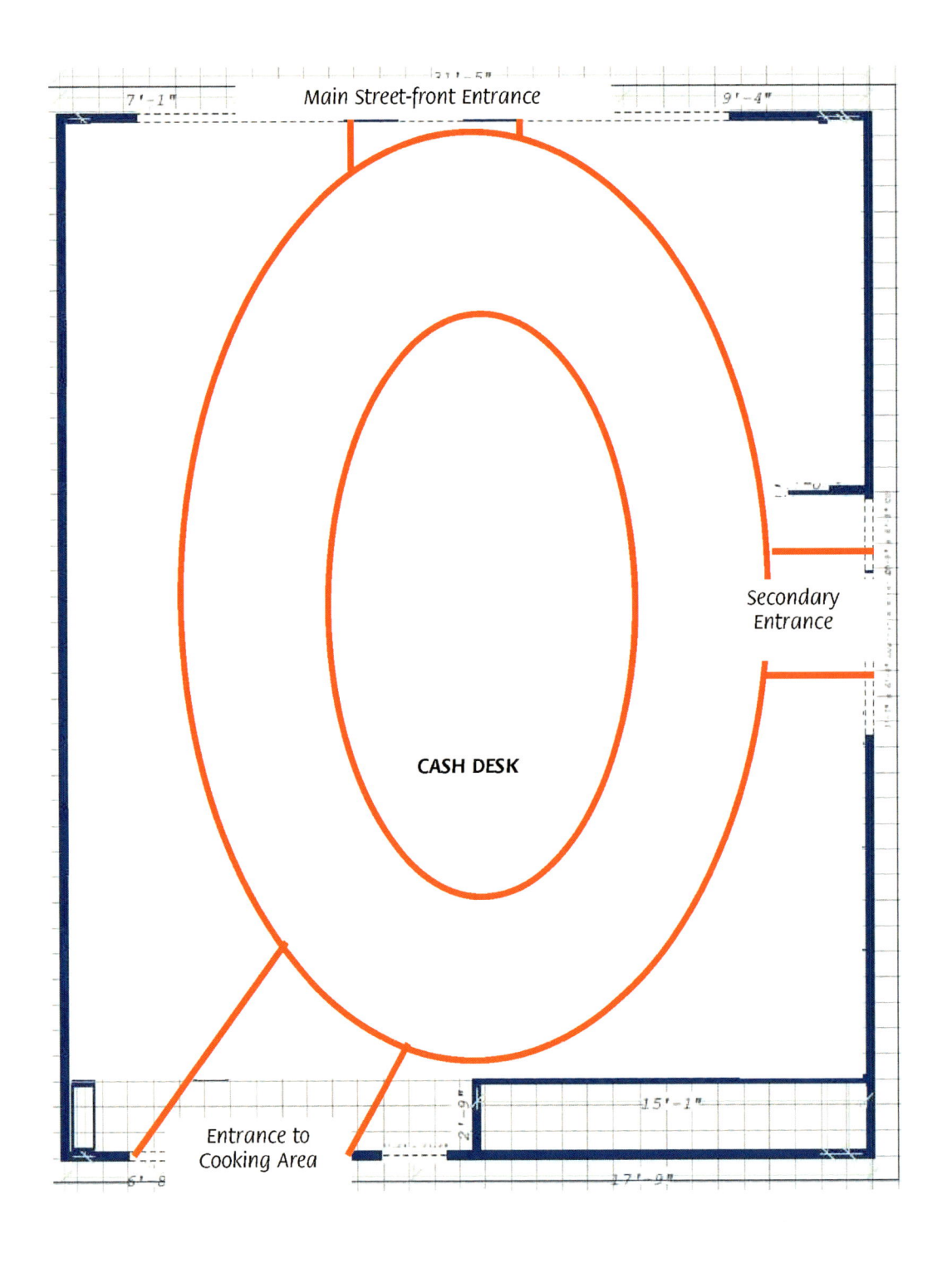

Planned merchandise categories are grouped and plotted in. While basics are normally located toward the back of a shop, in this case, the area with the least traffic will be the front left section. Customers walking toward the cooking school will take the shortest route on the right. Housing kitchen basics and food-to-go on the left makes these sections a destination. Exciting new features are located in the centre. Higher margin items such as appliances and brand name tableware complete the right section.

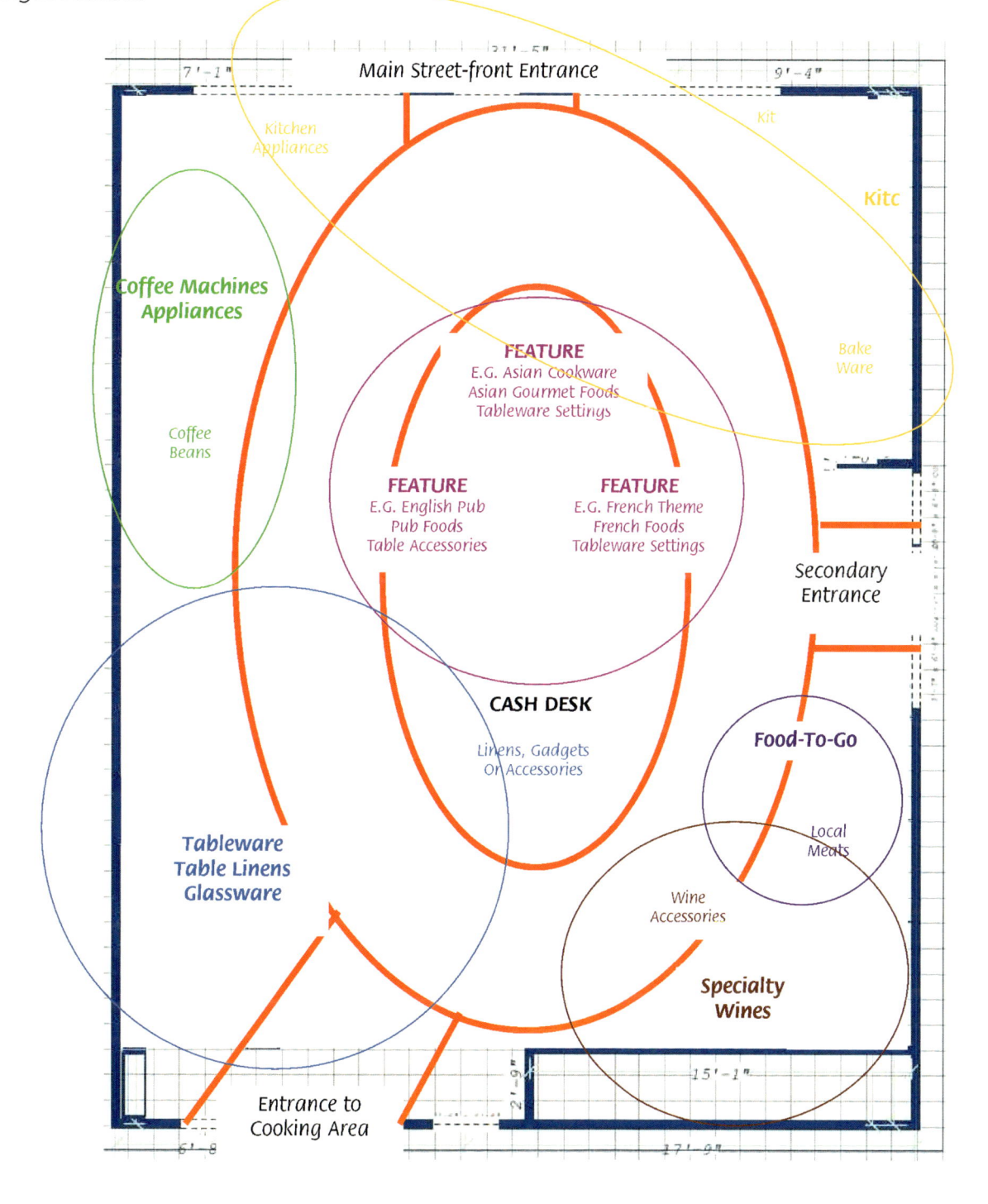

Main Street-front Entrance

- Kitchen Appliances
- Kitc
- Bake Ware
- Coffee Machines Appliances
- Coffee Beans
- **FEATURE** E.G. Asian Cookware / Asian Gourmet Foods / Tableware Settings
- **FEATURE** E.G. English Pub / Pub Foods / Table Accessories
- **FEATURE** E.G. French Theme / French Foods / Tableware Settings
- Secondary Entrance
- **CASH DESK**
- Linens, Gadgets or Accessories
- Tableware / Table Linens / Glassware
- Food-To-Go
- Local Meats
- Wine Accessories
- Specialty Wines
- Entrance to Cooking Area

STEP 2: FIXTURES PLACEMENT
Modular Fixtures = Less Headaches

There isn't serious talk about layout without significant fixture discussion. Along with columns and walls, fixtures determine layout. What type should you use? My constant answer works for all retail: the ones that offer the most flexibility. Often the least expensive fixtures offer the most modularity. While styles may vary, even top-end custom made ones use basic standards and fittings.

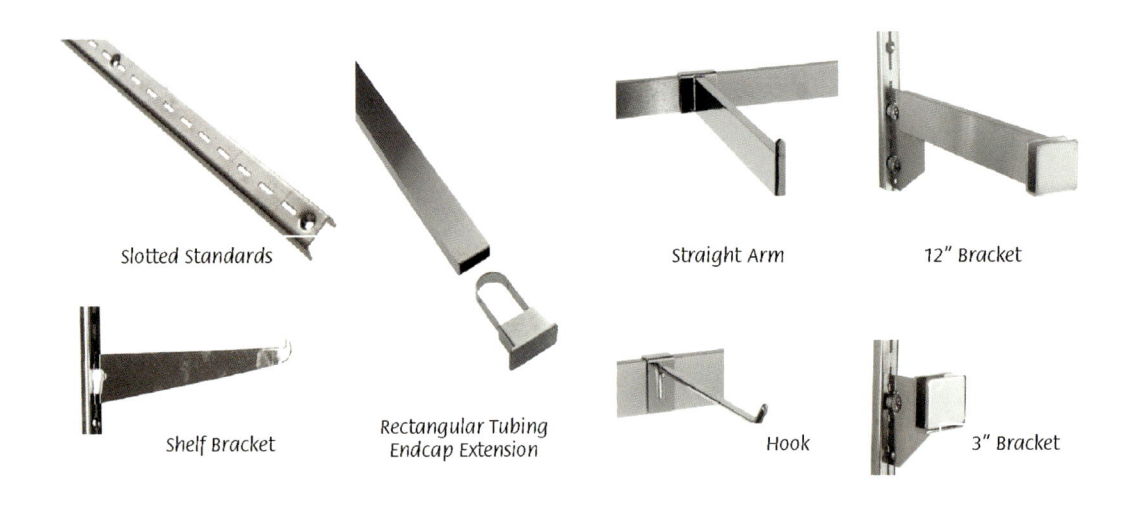

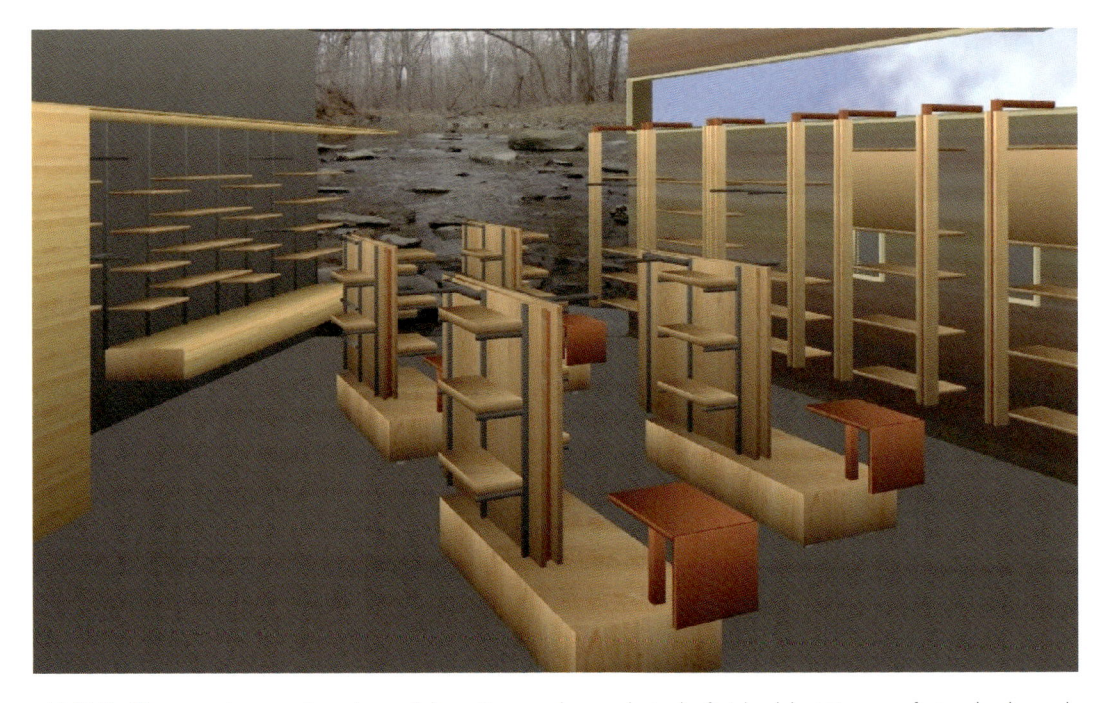

Slotted Standards

Straight Arm

12" Bracket

Shelf Bracket

Rectangular Tubing Endcap Extension

Hook

3" Bracket

ABOVE: These custom wall and gondola units may be exclusively finished but its use of standards and fittings are basic.

Basic standards and fittings are applied in the diagram below.
For a specific breakdown of standards and fittings, a planogram accompanies the 3D diagram.

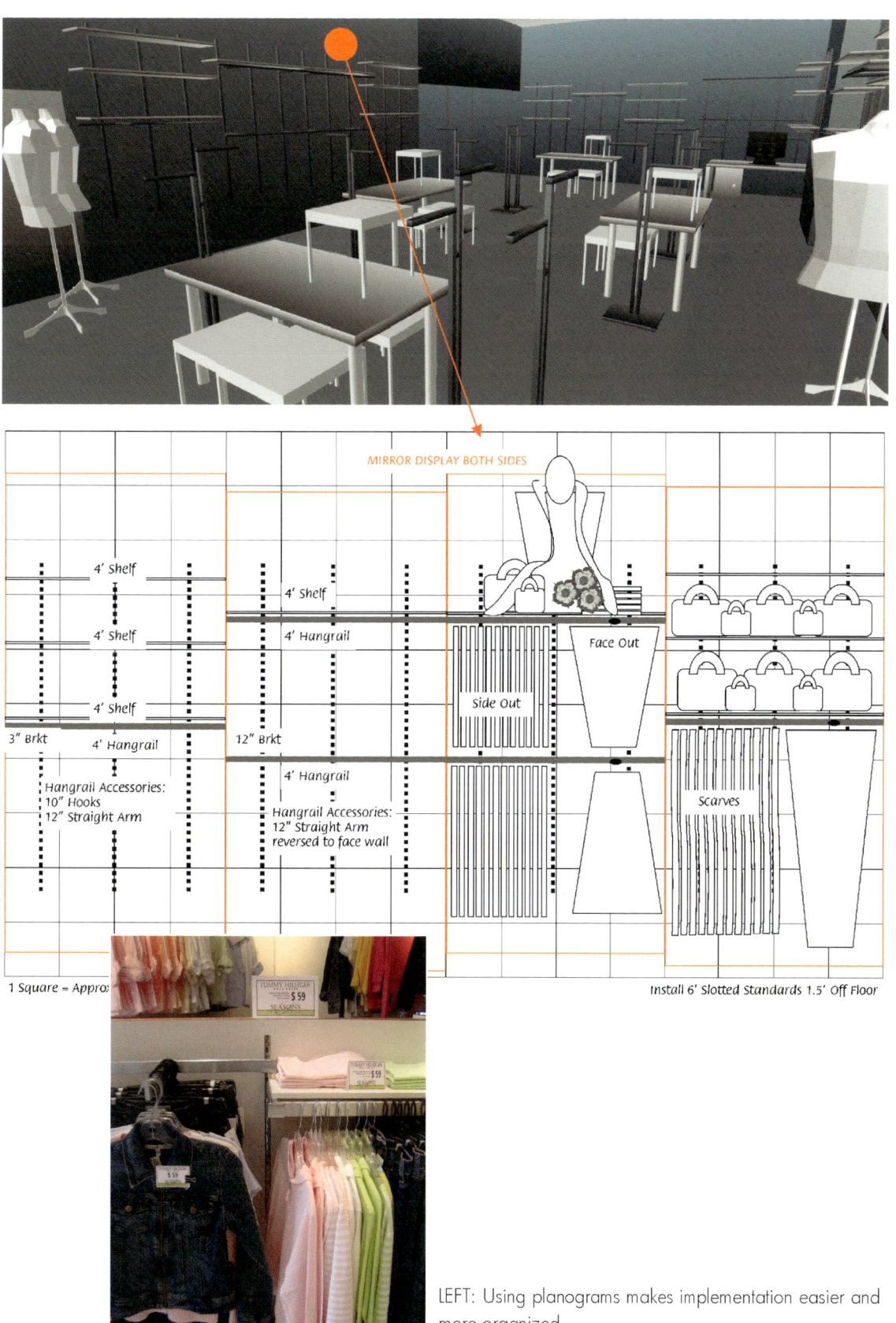

MIRROR DISPLAY BOTH SIDES

4' Shelf
4' Shelf
4' Shelf
3" Brkt   4' Hangrail
Hangrail Accessories:
10" Hooks
12" Straight Arm

4' Shelf
4' Hangrail
12" Brkt
4' Hangrail
Hangrail Accessories:
12" Straight Arm reversed to face wall

Face Out
Side Out
Scarves

1 Square = Approx

Install 6' Slotted Standards 1.5' Off Floor

LEFT: Using planograms makes implementation easier and more organized.

What's the story on Grids and slatwalls? Try to avoid slatwalls. While they offer versatility and are readily available in the market, their make-up presents a busy background. The goal for all merchandise presentation is to ensure that product is the 'star' of the show. Plan for very little distraction from the objects being sold. Slatwalls show dominant and repetitive slats that become too strong for most merchandise. The design is also not meant to carry heavy merchandise, unless reinforced with metal inserts. If you have slatwalls, lessen the visual impact by painting the entire board, including the inside. An alternative is to fill in the entire space with products or use backings to break up the lines.

BELOW LEFT: Slatwall

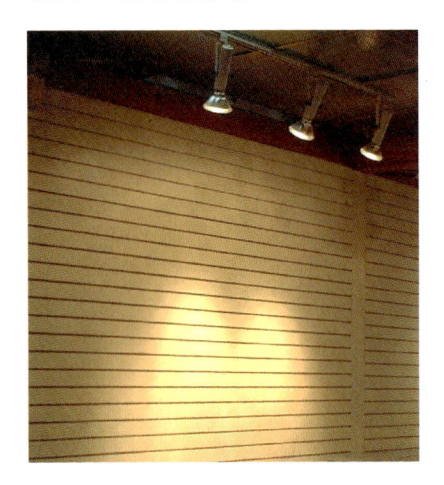

BELOW RIGHT: Grid Panel

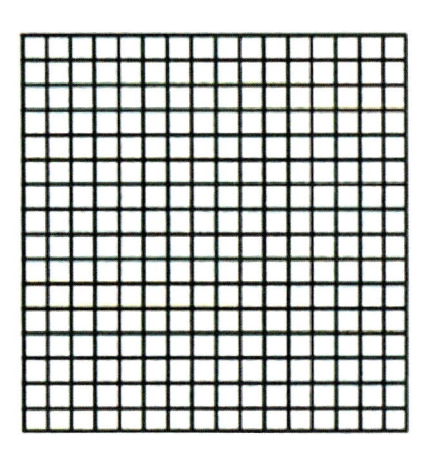

PHOTO BELOW: Fabric is used to break up the visually repetitive lines in this slatwall display.

How do you determine fixture type? As a general rule, fixtures should start low in front, and be higher in the back. In large shops, perspective changes depending on where aisles are located, however this guideline still applies.

ABOVE: From storefront to back or from floor units to the wall, fixtures gradually increase in height. This leads the eye from the front to the back wall.

LEFT: Heavenly Outhouse of Cochrane, Alberta illustrates how a display can lead the eye from front to back. This is achieved by placing low fixtures closest to a customers' viewing point and tall units far back against the wall.

The most often used fixtures are:
NESTING TABLES

Nesting Tables provide an interesting display because they invite the eye to travel up and down. The top table can house a focal display while the bottom ones carry merchandise. Tables can be rectangular, square, round or oblong. Many of my clients have success with Ikea's Vika Amon (top right photo) or Vika Manne tables, and either Lack coffee tables or Klubbo tables (top left & right photos).

Small retailers value Ikea's price, design and quick availability. I expect some might comment on this recommendation, or more specifically, question whether the quality can withstand 50 years of store operation. In reality, the cost and shape are ideal, and strength is sufficient. Keep in mind fixture pieces generally need updating after about 5 years, irregardless.

LEFT PHOTO: A nesting effect is achieved with the use of Ikea's Vika Manne Round tables with Kaj adjustable legs.

GONDOLA UNITS

There are many different designs for Gondolas. Most often, they contain at least a back panel to hold merchandise up on either side. Some have side panels as well, allowing for more stability and merchandising space. Sizes vary from a width of 4' to 8', or even at times, 12'. For small stores, I recommend nothing more than 6'.

ABOVE LEFT:
A gondola unit fitted with basic standards offers Seasons Fashions of Whitehorse a versatile way to merchandise a clothing collection.
ABOVE RIGHT:
An Ikea Expedit bookcase is set upon a platform to showcase Vancouver's Drinkwater & Company's home accessory pieces.

SHELVING UNITS

Shelving Units provide interest in any store setting. Fashion apparel, home accessories, toys, specialty food - these are only a few merchandise types that benefit from shelving units. I've recommended bookcase units such as Ikea's Expedit or Billy. Not only do they stand on their own, they can be built into walls or integrated with other pieces for a more custom look. There are also many different varieties and finishes available to suit your store design. Open shelving units such as Ikea's Norrebo can also double as a section divider.

T-STANDS

For fashion apparel, T-Stands offer the most flexibility. They can stand independently or be grouped in 2's or 3's. This is a great unit to use for 'onesies' or 'twosies' mixed in with coordinating colour groups, without losing perceived value. T-Stands usually come with one waterfall arm and one straight arm. The waterfall arm is meant to be used for tops while straight arms for bottoms. I recommend 2 straight arms for a cleaner look. (Bottom left photo)

4-WAY RACKS

Along with T-Stands, 4-Ways are one of the most common units seen in fashion stores. The front arm is usually a waterfall while the rest are straight arms. The 4-Way makes a good fashion statement for coordinating pieces. For example, the waterfall arm can merchandise jackets, the 2 side arms may house blouses or tops on one, and skirts on the other. The back arm displays pants. The 4-Way has one limitation. Unless you have the complete coordinating pieces, either by story, fabrication or colour, the look may be less than stellar. I recommend 2 T-stands side by side, working as a 4-Way, for more flexibility.
(Photos above right shows a standard 4-Way and a Multi-level 4-Way)

ROUND RACKS

Rounders are great for sale merchandise. They often signal merchandise that is off-price or on sale, thus drawing customers. Another use for Rounders is to display product statements- such as a Rounder filled with one type of merchandise. Tri-level Rounders offer retailers a way to display related merchandise within one unit while keeping a clean and organized look. The lowest level usually fronts the customer, followed by the mid level to the right, and then the highest level at the left-back. For example, tank tops on the lowest level, short sleeved t-shirts on the mid, and long sleeved t-shirts on the tallest level. When merchandising colours, start from the 9 o'clock position and turning clockwise using rainbow colours. (Photo above right)

Other fixtures that work similarly to standards are the Outrigger System (photo below left), Ladder (below right) and Mini-Ladder Systems. They provide the same flexibility a Slotted Standard would.

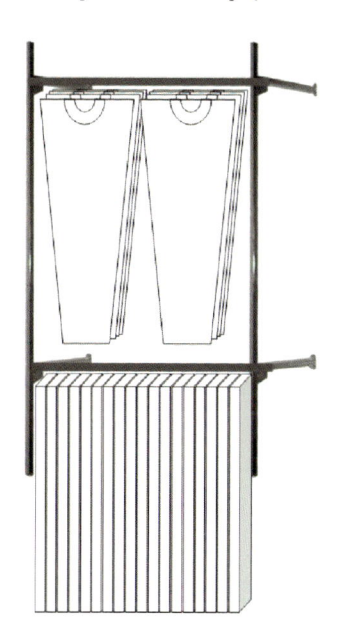

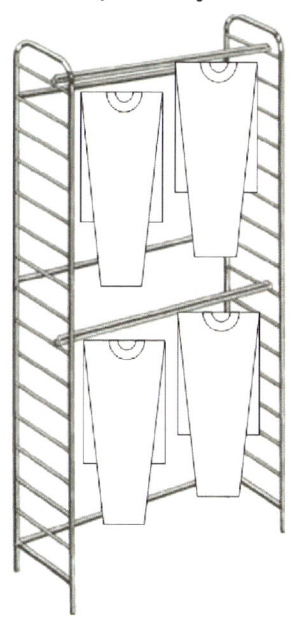

STEP 3: PUTTING IT ALL TOGETHER

An example of a basic sectional layout includes a set of nesting tables, two gondolas or sets of T-stands. With this in mind, verify the dimensions of the fixtures you've chosen and begin plotting this onto the graph. Ensure a minimum of 3' between fixtures for secondary aisles and 4' for main aisles.

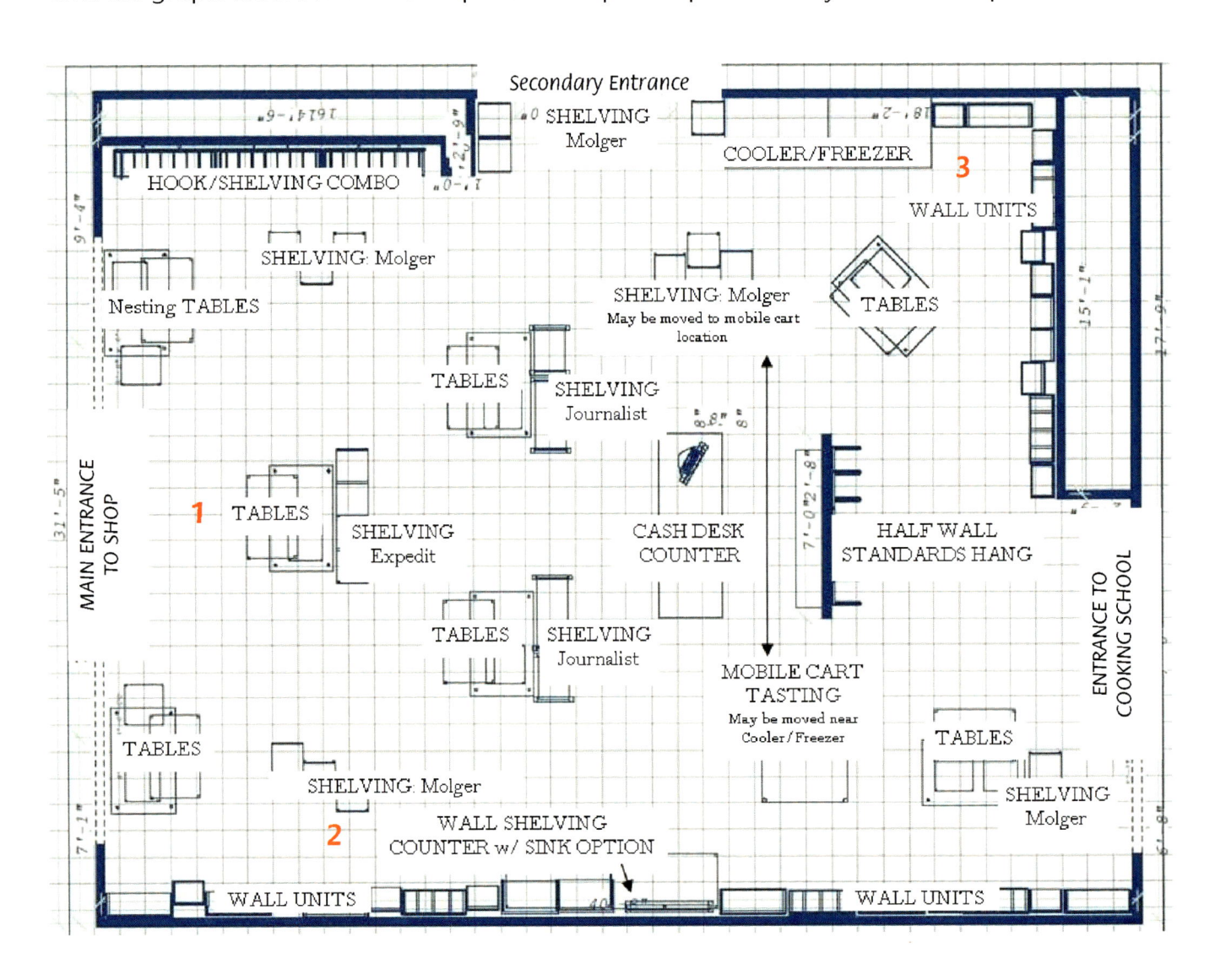

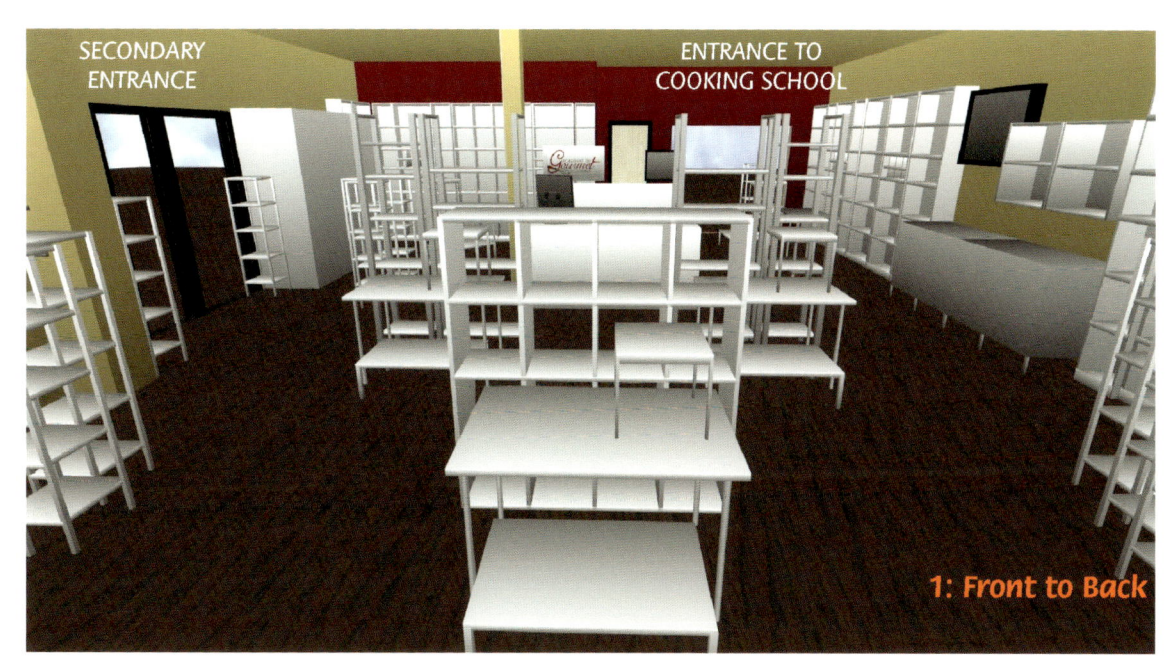

SECONDARY ENTRANCE

ENTRANCE TO COOKING SCHOOL

1: Front to Back

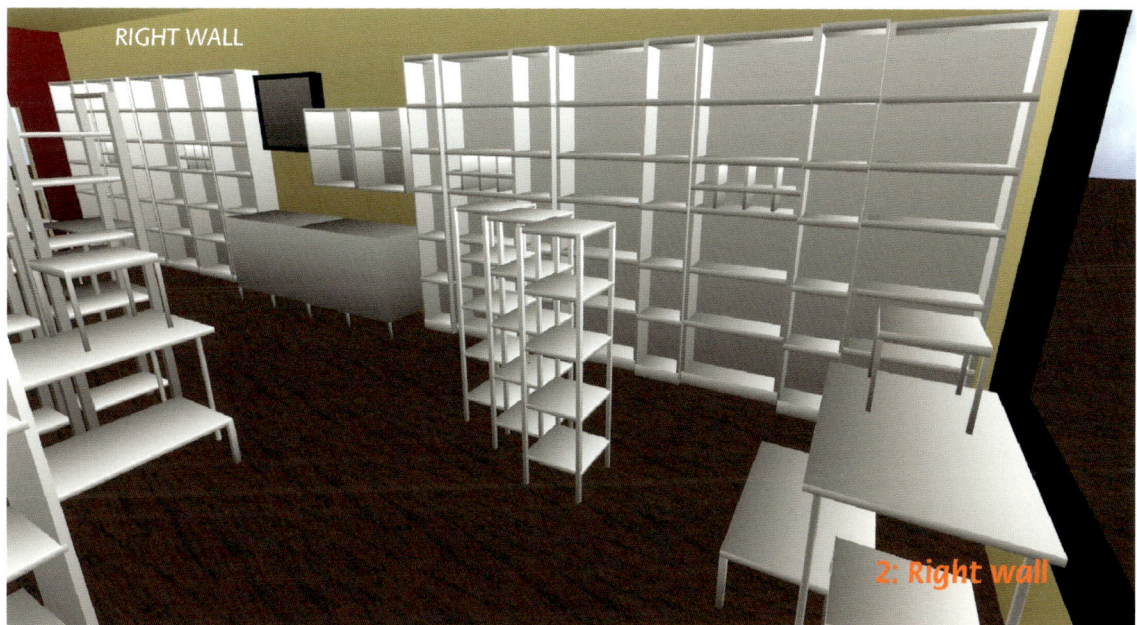

RIGHT WALL

2: Right Wall

MAIN ENTRANCE

3: Back to Front Entrance

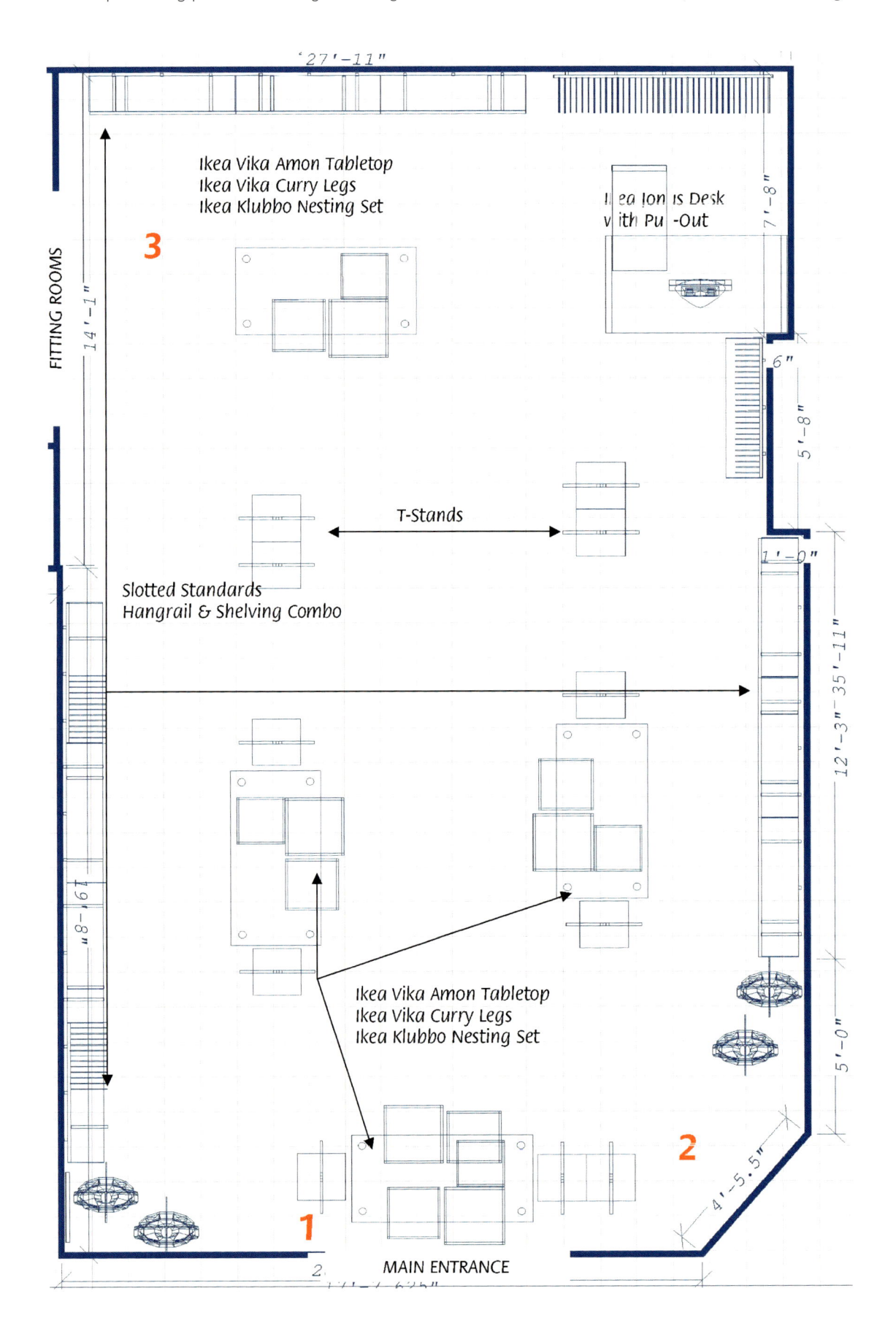

BELOW: A sample fixturing plan for a clothing store using a combination of wall Slotted standards, T-stands and Nesting Tables.

Ikea Vika Amon Tabletop
Ikea Vika Curry Legs
Ikea Klubbo Nesting Set

Ikea Jonas Desk with Pull-Out

T-Stands

Slotted Standards
Hangrail & Shelving Combo

Ikea Vika Amon Tabletop
Ikea Vika Curry Legs
Ikea Klubbo Nesting Set

FITTING ROOMS

MAIN ENTRANCE

60

BACK WALL

1: Front to Back

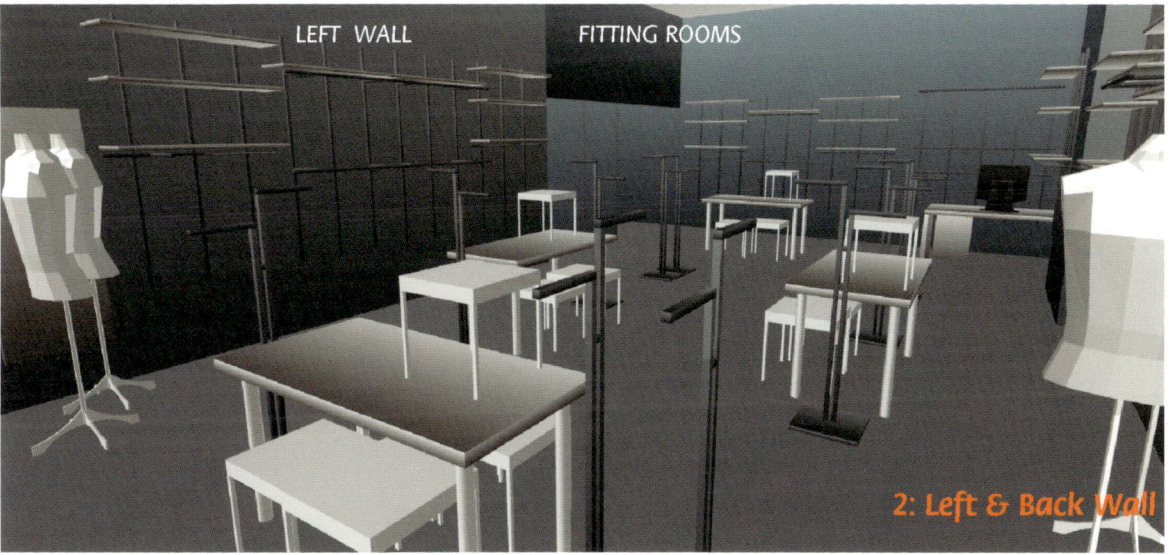

LEFT WALL   FITTING ROOMS

2: Left & Back Wall

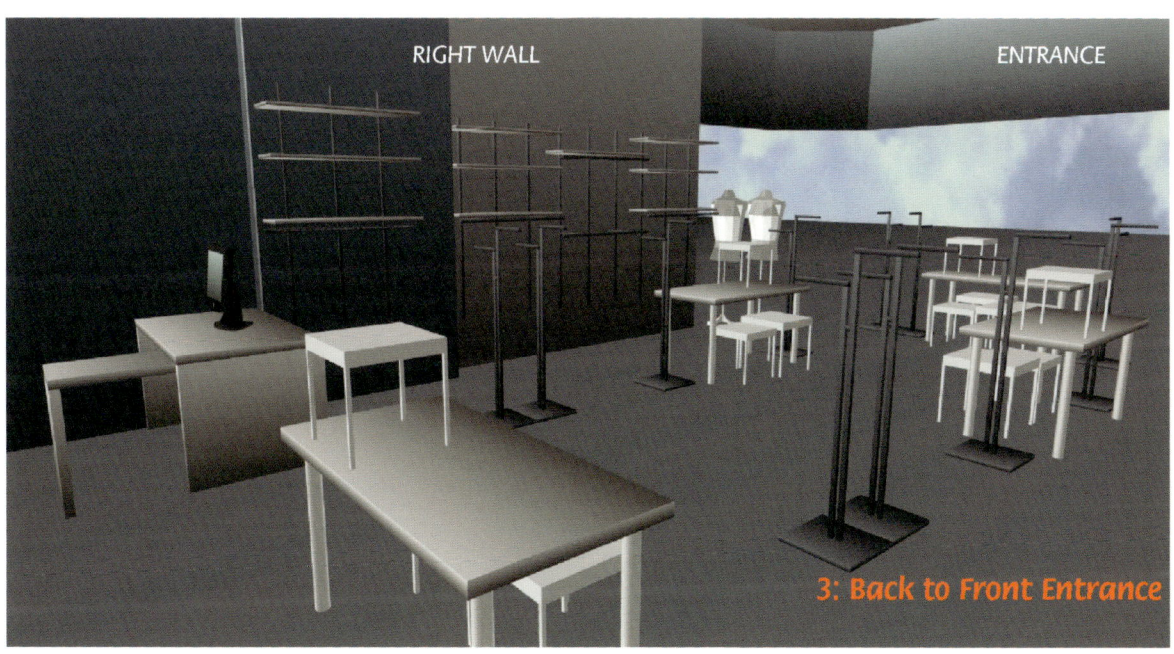

RIGHT WALL   ENTRANCE

3: Back to Front Entrance

STEP 4: IDENTIFYING STRIKE ZONES, POWER WALLS and FOCAL POINTS

STRIKE ZONES

Usually located in high traffic areas such aisle intersections, Strike Zones are areas that garner a good amount of attention. This is the natural place to display high margin goods or to introduce new merchandise stories. I often use Strike Zones to provide shop owners with a guideline to how much merchandise stories they can carry.

POWER WALLS

What are power walls and what do they do? Power walls are effective tools. Retailers can use them to attract customers into the store, or to propel them towards the back, increasing penetration. Any wall can become a power wall. Designate a single theme or dominant story for a compelling merchandise presentation that captures customers. Most stores select walls adjacent to the entrance as Power Walls because it allows the primary story to be conveyed effectively. Back walls also make great Power Walls as they entice customers further inside the store.

A variety of merchandise types may be used to build Power Walls. Near the entrance, fashion retailers usually display the season's new arrivals. This Power Wall (or story wall) conveys the store's image, intended customer and the prominent merchandise story. A bookshop may use such a Power Wall to display the top 10 bestsellers or new releases. Large format value retailers and home/hardware stores display seasonal merchandise. Lawn and garden products build summer Power Walls, and festive accessories during the holiday season. For a casual clothing shop, the back wall may serve as a power wall that displays all types of jeans. There are endless applications. The key for retailers is to tap into the "power" to increase capture and conversion (sales). (Sample Power Wall photo facing page.)

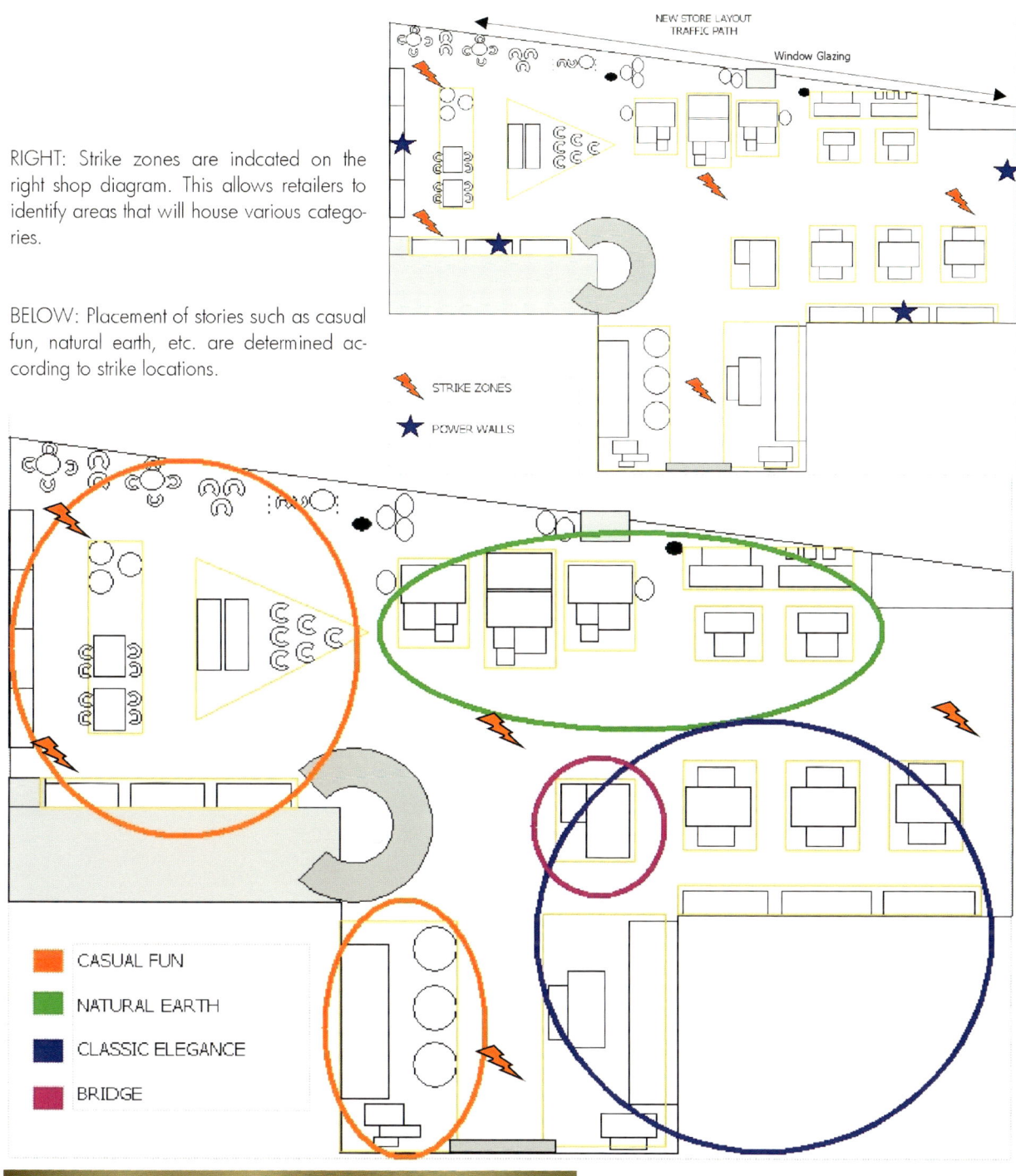

RIGHT: Strike zones are indicated on the right shop diagram. This allows retailers to identify areas that will house various categories.

BELOW: Placement of stories such as casual fun, natural earth, etc. are determined according to strike locations.

⚡ STRIKE ZONES
★ POWER WALLS

- CASUAL FUN
- NATURAL EARTH
- CLASSIC ELEGANCE
- BRIDGE

LEFT: A sample power wall shows the dominant merchandise story. It shares similar design, fabrication and more importantly, targets the same customer.

63

FOCAL POINTS

Focal Points are the "showcases" of a store. This is where the stage is set. The play (display) draws customers to the product. Natural Focal Points direct attention by virtue of their size, such as columns or other architectural elements. These areas make for great visual display locations.

Ideally, each section will contain a primary or main focal display atop a nesting table or in the front area of the department. A secondary focal point, usually on a wall, draws customers further into the store. Focal displays on walls break the monotony of its length. Usually placed 8' apart, focal points can be created through product displays or signs and graphics.

LEFT: The main focal display on the left draws the eye from the front all the way to the back wall.

TOP PHOTO: Secondary focal displays on the top most shelf unit draw the eye down to merchandise housed beneath it.

64

LAYOUT EXERCISE 1

Start by drawing 2 sidewalls and a back wall. Then play with different fixture positions for this newsstand. Where would you want to put the cash desk? For this exercise, don't worry about exact sizes and floor space. The aim is to get comfortable with moving fixtures around in order to yield the best sales results. Fixtures different from those shown below may be used.

Once you decide on your final layout, indicate any power walls, strike zones and focal points.

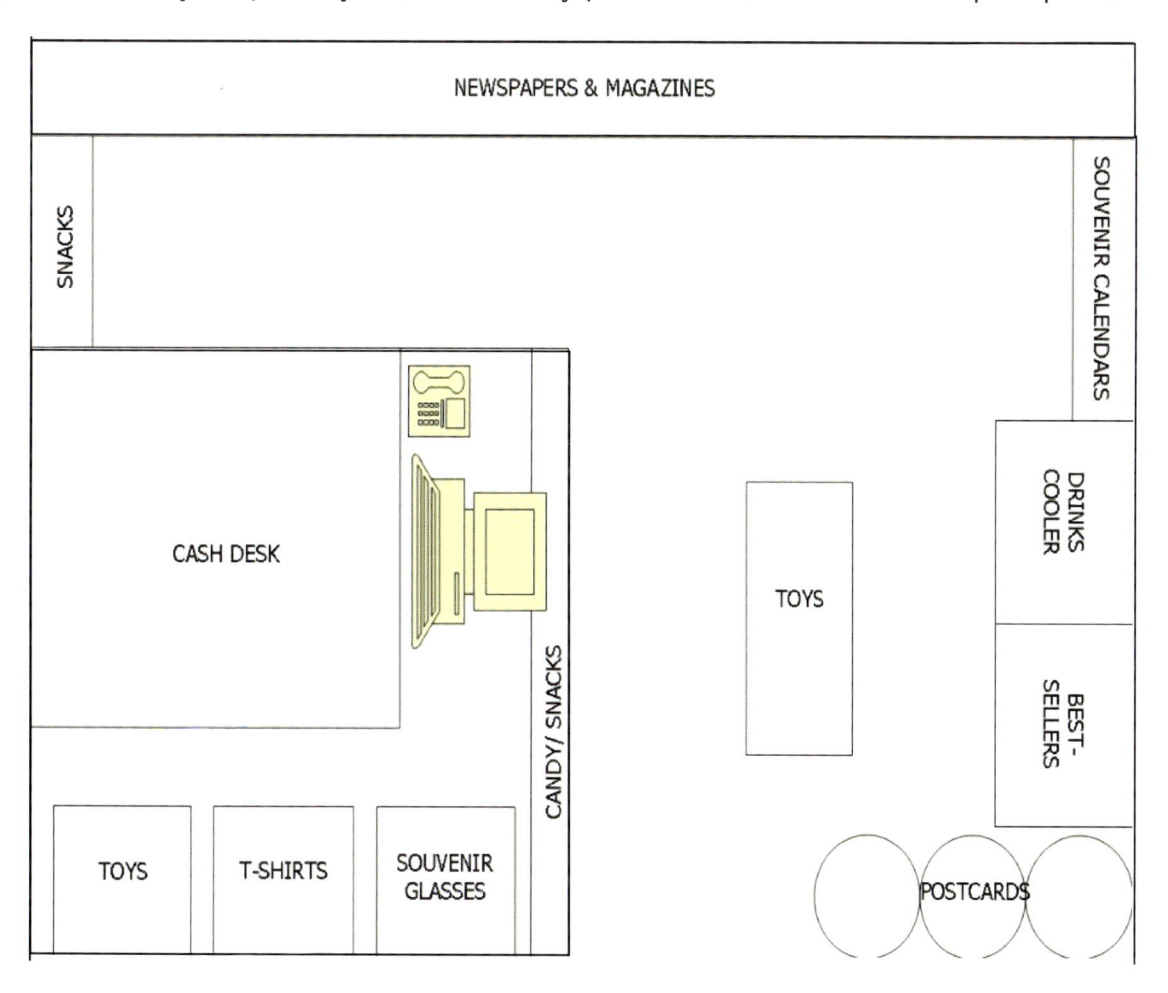

NEWSPAPERS & MAGAZINES

SNACKS

SOUVENIR CALENDARS

CASH DESK

DRINKS COOLER

TOYS

BEST-SELLERS

CANDY/SNACKS

TOYS | T-SHIRTS | SOUVENIR GLASSES

POSTCARDS

ENTRANCE

LAYOUT EXERCISE 2

Troubleshooting

Customers in this Gift shop browse only the right of the store, seldom walking to the back and around to the left. Can you find a better way to layout store fixtures to open up the selling space? The cash section takes up the left front section. The selling space is 22.5' deep and about 9' wide. Walls are lined with shelving units and a set of nesting table rests at the back wall. There are 3 card spinners standing in the middle of the shop. Try this exercise using the grid sheet on the following page. Each square equals a square foot of the store.

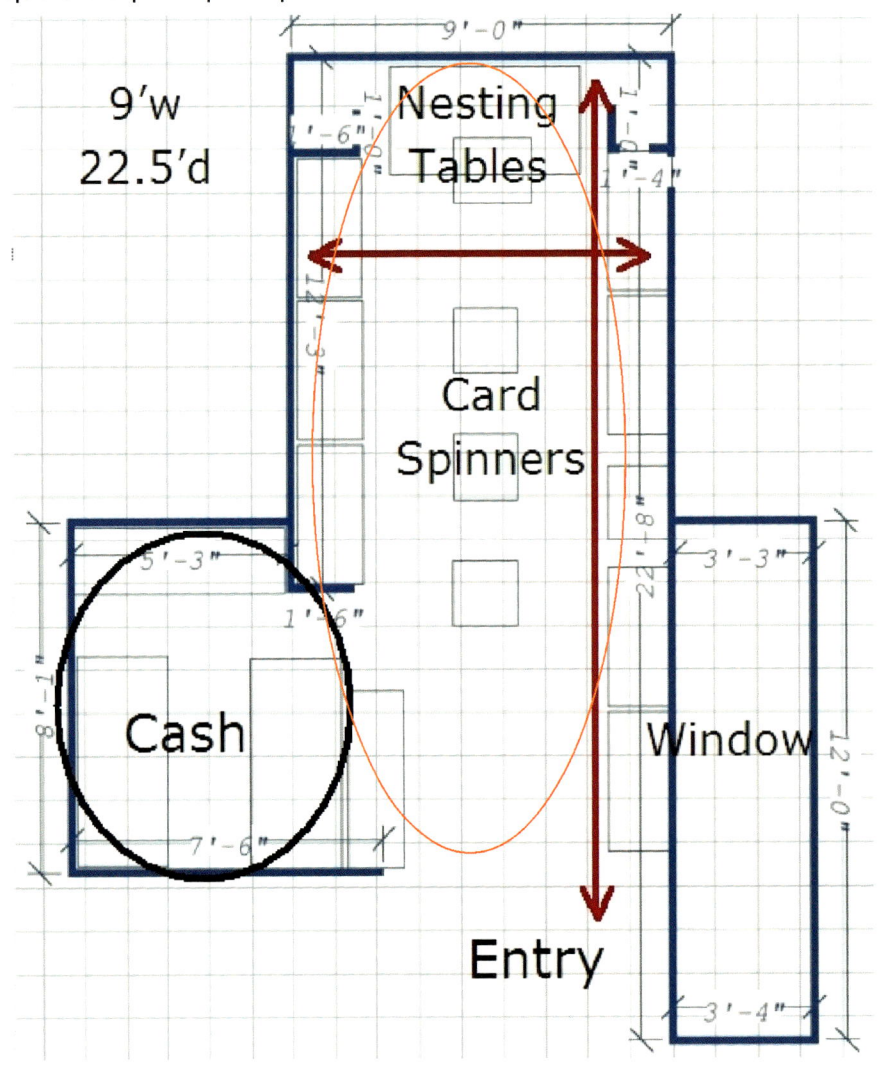

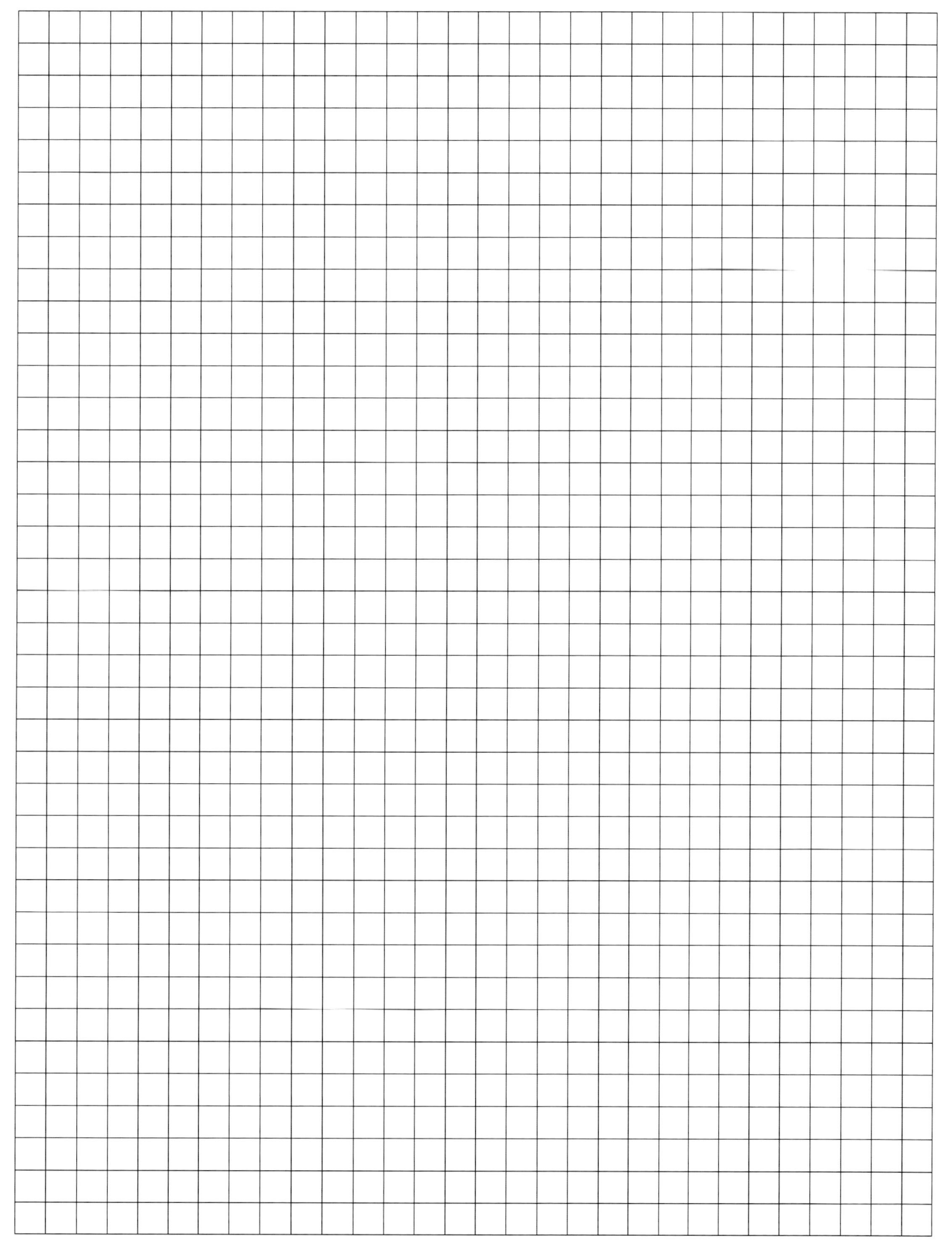

LAYOUT CASE STUDY: Color O Living (HOME DÉCOR)
BEATING THE POST-HOLIDAY BLUES

" Ever since implementing visual strategies in our store, sales have increased 61% and we've experienced 140% increase in units productivity."

David Lui, Past President Thomson and Fenn Trading
Aberdeen Centre, Richmond, BC, Canada

Sales increase after the holiday season???
Most retailers' sales plunge after the holiday rush. Color O Living, a home accessories shop at Aberdeen Centre, enjoyed a surge. Unusual? An increase in sales by 61% —unbelievable? Well, believe it! Numbers speak for themselves. David Lui, then President of Thomson and Fenn Trading, operated Color O Living. He believes, "atmospherics played into at least 90% of the increase in sales."

The power of store atmospherics lies in influence. How do customers view and move? Starting with store layout, we watched how customers walked the entire store to give us clues on how to create a more effective layout. For Color O Living, it was more a case of where customers didn't walk. An improved layout would ensure full store penetration.

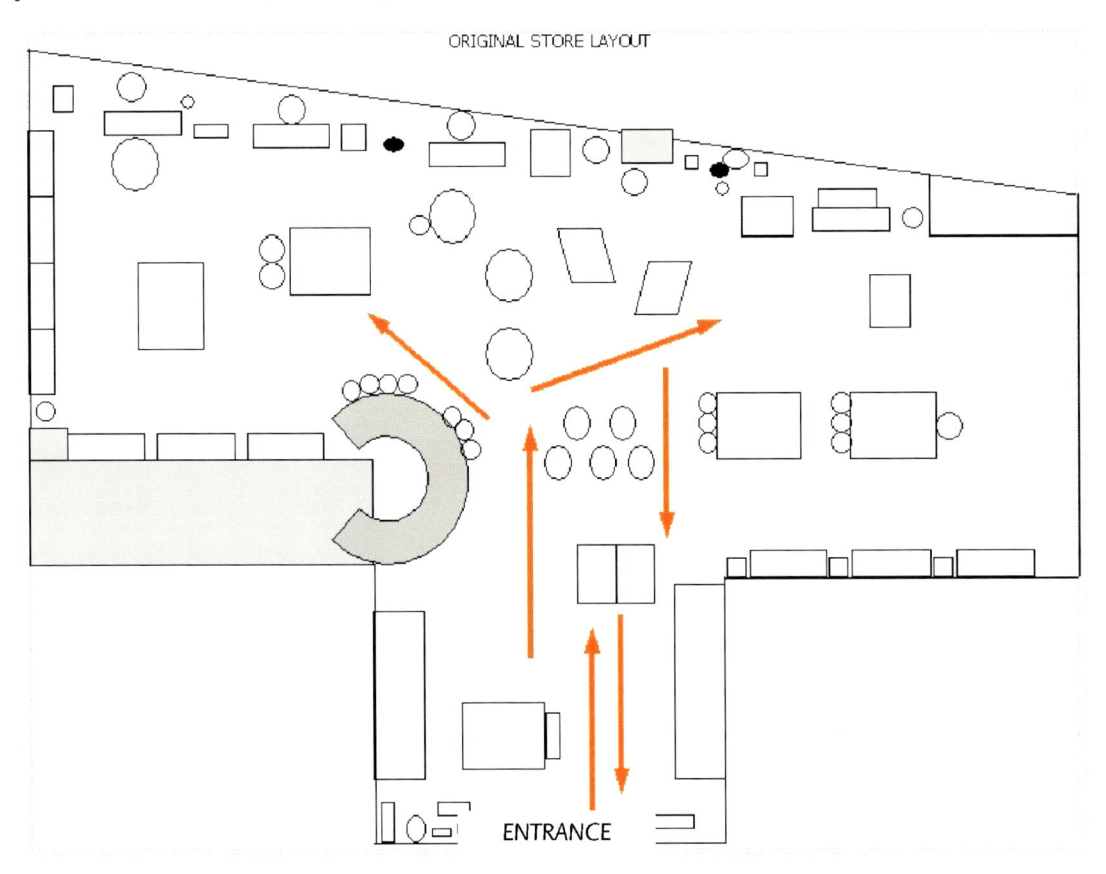

ABOVE DIAGRAM:
The original layout failed to provide customers with a convenient walkway to view the entire shop display. Most entered, looked to the left and right, then boomeranged out the shop. (See arrows)

CASE STUDY: Color O Living (HOME DÉCOR) continued
BEATING THE POST-HOLIDAY BLUES

The diagram in the previous page shows the 'before' layout, with directional arrows indicating how customers walked through the store. Fixtures were placed haphazardly with little thought as to how customers would navigate the selling space.

The diagram below shows the new layout and how the store is currently shopped. Nesting tables were brought in and grouped to create distinctive merchandise stories.

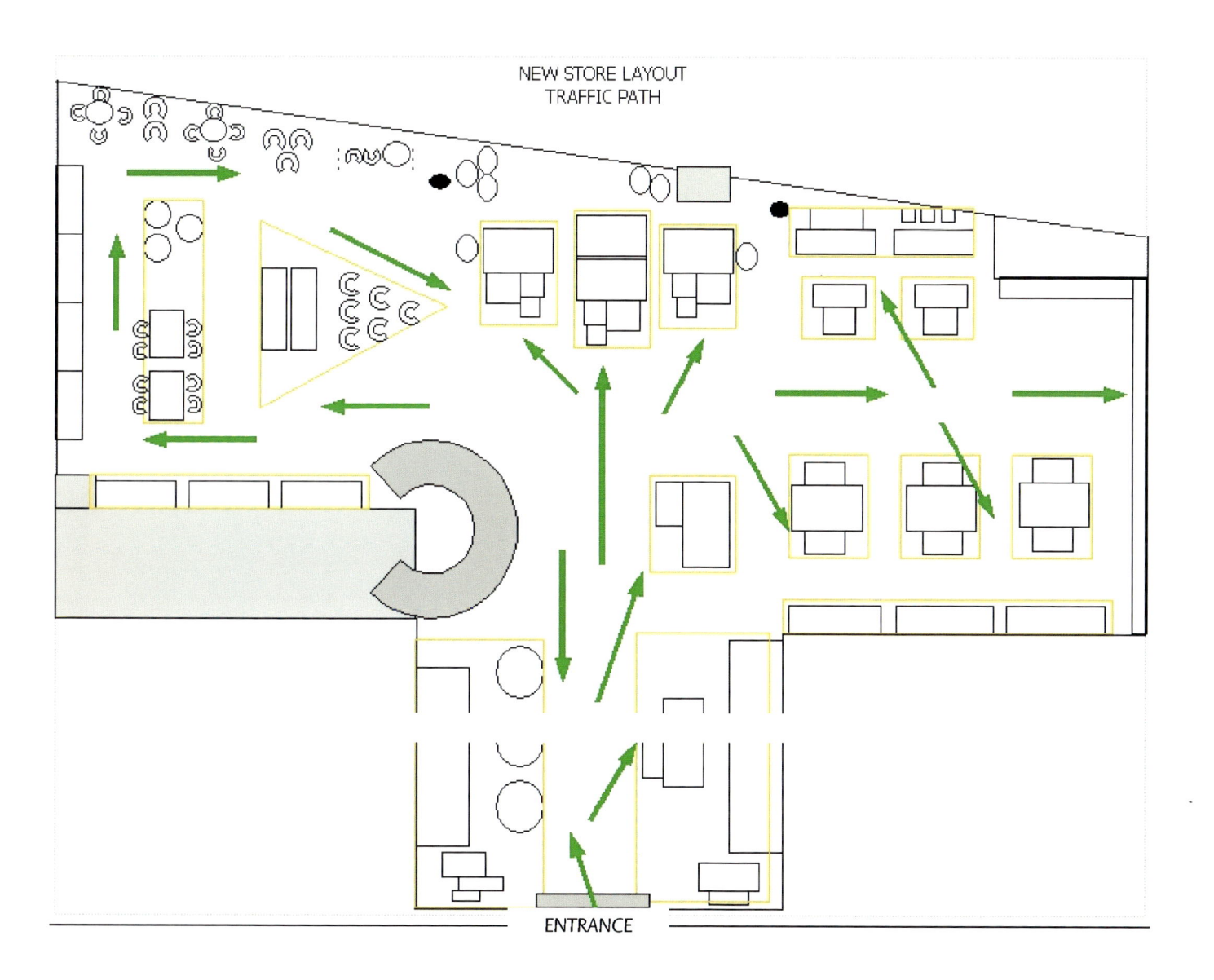

NEW STORE LAYOUT
TRAFFIC PATH

ENTRANCE

LEFT COLUMN PHOTOS: Pre-Transformation
RIGHT COLUMN PHOTOS: Post-Transformation
New displays attract customer interest while re-using old fixtures helped keep operations within budget during this transformation.

70

Answer Key: Layout Exercise 1

PROPOSED NEW LAYOUT

A defined racetrack makes shopping easy and convenient in this newsstand. With a central cash desk, customers are encouraged to shop the walls where majority of the merchandise is displayed. A back Power Wall of reading materials draw customers to the all the way into the shop.

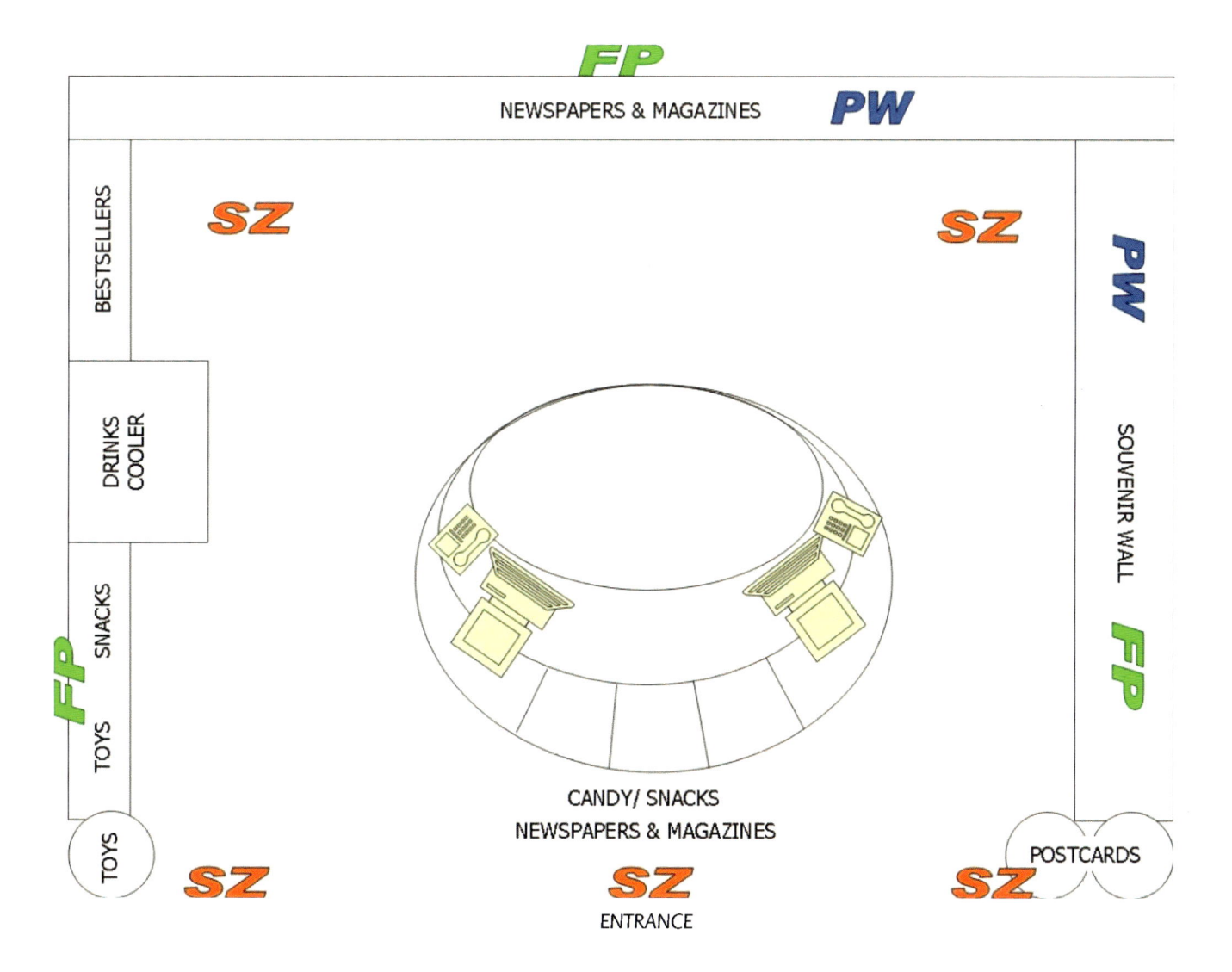

FP
NEWSPAPERS & MAGAZINES **PW**

BESTSELLERS **SZ** **SZ** **PW**

DRINKS COOLER

FP SNACKS

TOYS SOUVENIR WALL **FP**

TOYS

CANDY/ SNACKS
NEWSPAPERS & MAGAZINES
POSTCARDS
SZ **SZ** **SZ**
ENTRANCE

Note that higher margin souvenir items are placed to the right of the shop, while destination items such as food-to-go are on the left. Toys are merchandised upfront to appeal to children. Impulse items surround the cash desk.

Answer Key: Layout Exercise 2

PROPOSED NEW LAYOUT:

The new layout below moves the cash section to the back of the store, thereby making the selling space shallower. This opens up the front left section as selling space, resulting in a wider space up front; about 14.5' wide. Shop depth was reduced from 22.5' to 14.5'.

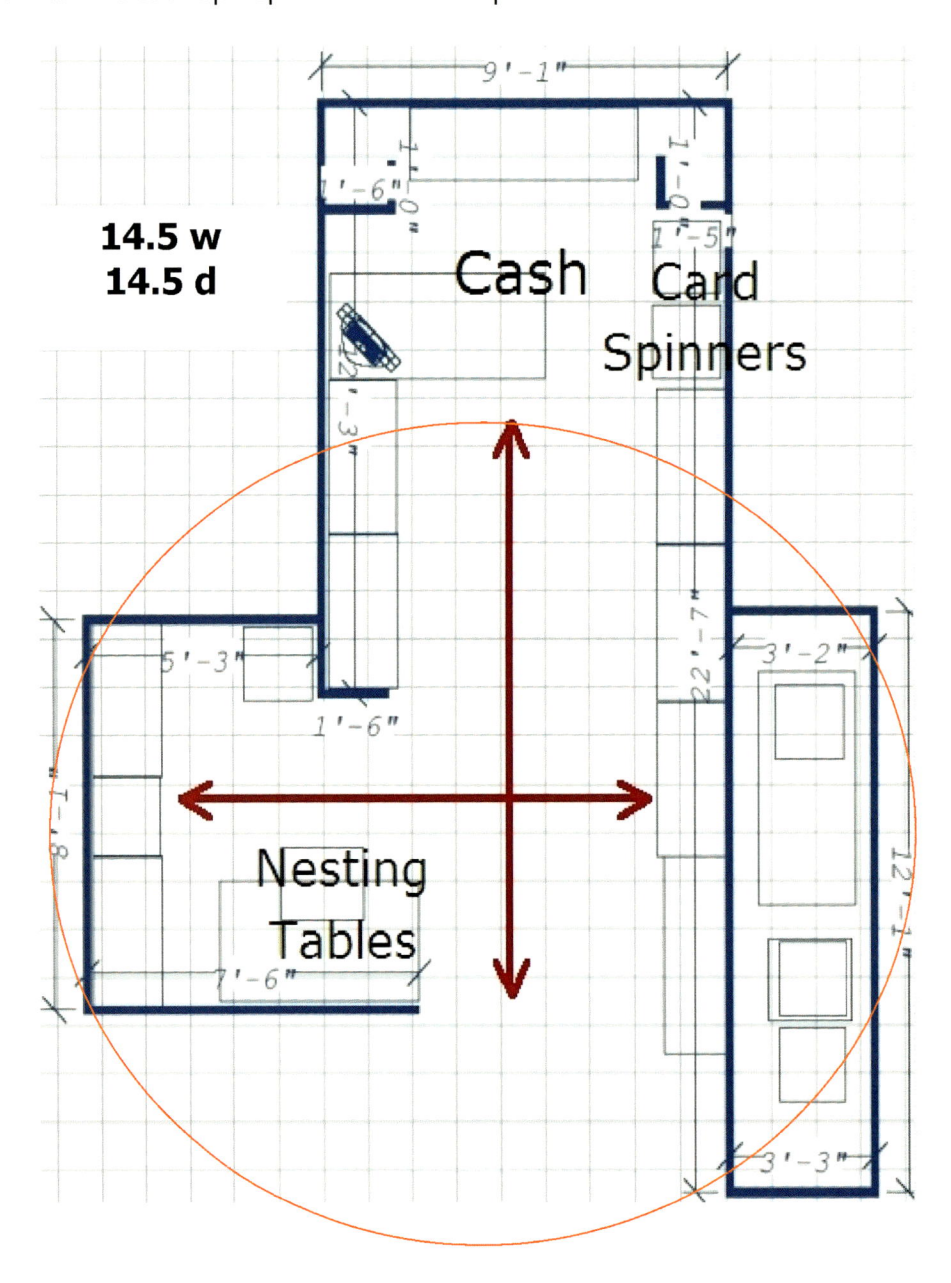

14.5 w
14.5 d

Cash   Card Spinners

Nesting Tables

View this shop's before and after photos next page.

72

As a small retailer in Richmond's Pacific Plaza, The Caring Shop provides its young audience a venue to make new friends and equip them with relational tools such as caring gifts and training workshops. According to Alan Yu, the store manager, the gift shop "brings good quality items with good design at a good price". For this project, Alan wanted to ensure that this small gift shop become a profit center for the company, one that not only provides the goods his customers want but also ensured that all selling opportunities are maximized.

This project was completed at the end of September 2005. In the month following, sales went up 221% over the same time last year. Sales per transaction increased by 26% and the number of walk-in customers went up 40%. (Retail Connections, January 2006)

TOP: Pre-Transformation
RIGHT: Post-Transformation

73

STAGE THE HAPPY ENDING
What to Put Where, Why and How
Category Adjacency Plan & Displays

Create A Happy Ending

At Gift Shows retailers often ask where to place things they've just purchased. Up front? At the back or by the cash counter? Incorporating new products with merchandise stories already in store brings about important considerations. Retailers need to contemplate which items will be most effective next to each other.

The right placements lie in understanding Product Adjacency principles. In the last chapter, we examined how traffic flow is influenced by aisle placement as well as wall and floor fixtures. In this section, we will discuss the importance of the Product Adjacency factor. Where products are situated ties into exposure, and its role in determining buying.

Come up with an Adjacency Plan that controls which merchandise story is presented first as customers walk inside. It will include what products are grouped together. A plan also determines the last thing people see as they exit.

Certain categories placed next to each other maximize all selling opportunities. Market research provides ample proof of this trend. Use the Adjacency Plan to tailor your merchandise set-up according to current business needs. For example, door crashers, loss leader sales, seasonal drives or feature stories that support current marketing drives can be grouped together.

Setting The Stage

Imagine your store as the script for a play. The exterior represents the stage set, with store name and logo as its opening act. Ask yourself - the playwright or stage director - what message do you wish to convey by the storefront window presentation. Does the title and cover design grab attention? Is it interesting enough to invite readers in? Make bold decisions and work to compose an interesting story. Build themes around price points, selection or lifestyle.

Your Role As Director

Lights, Camera …. Action! Let's say you've set the stage upfront. A customer walks inside, and then scans the store from left to right. At this point, the shopper is past the front cover and into the Introduction. Utilize strategies that help guide customers along the shopping experience, with a cleverly crafted plot called the Adjacency Plan.

As the shopper walks the path you've set, introduce your first merchandise category or story. What follows must be a seamless transition from one chapter on to the next, and the next. Each chapter has the potential to draw a shopper closer to a happy ending we'll call the point of sale. With the help of an efficient Adjacency Plan, you can enjoy a brilliant encore of successful sales.

Merchandise As Stage Props

An effective focal display in store helps create "rising action". This is a big part of invoking the desire to purchase. Make sure to display merchandise in an interesting and attention-getting fashion. Products displayed properly are the ultimate prop and will lead customers to the "climax" scene, when the cash register goes **ka-chingg!**

Realize the importance of your role as a stage director or playwright. The whole shopping experience can be choreographed by setting a scene (your store is your stage, your products are the props), creating a good plot (a chain of reactions you want customers to experience), and providing a lineup of remarkable characters (store associates).

Know Your Audience

Let's back up a little. The first move in determining categories or merchandise 'stories' is a step back. Find out about your customers' shopping priorities. This involves knowing what their lifestyle is like. It takes into consideration personal preferences for colour, style and utility.

Let's examine a home accessory store, as an example, to find out how the Adjacency Plan can be utilized to set the stage. Remember, deciding what to put where, how and why will eventually influence customers. This is the way to increase chances of your merchandise finding its way to a proud new owner.

Most home accessories stores display inventory by end use. This involves grouping major categories by location or 'room'. End use marketing shows customers how the product will fit in their home and what it will look like among other furnishing elements.

As playwright or stage director, make your statement using a unique presentation right away at the storefront window. Attract a captive audience with an introductory theme that makes the right impression. Depending on inventory and customer preference, the first group presented is the "Living Room" story. When a guest enters your home, the living room is usually the first to be shown.

Use the slice-of-life technique. Follow the "Living Room" scene by a "Dining Room" story, and then "Kitchen and Bath". In order to help create and maintain customer interest, ensure that storyline and plot take the customer seamlessly from one chapter or product category to the next.

ADJANCENCY PLAN & DISPLAY CASE STUDY 1: Drinkwater & Co

Merchandising by stories is beneficial in many ways. First, this is what differentiates retailers from each other, even if they carry exactly the same products. One retailer may tell a story on Romance using flowers while another may tell a story of 'Home as a Retreat' using the very same flowers. Second, customers love to find 'treasures' while shopping. In fact, most women pride themselves in being great treasure hunters. Displaying products by stories allows customers to experience the thrill of finding treasures that draw them further into your story telling. They can envision the product in an atmosphere that they can relate to, something that tugs at their hearts, which brings us to the third benefit. Stories make an immediate emotional connection. The presentation, the music, the scent surrounding the display sets the stage for drama that engages the customer in a deeper level. One that is warm and inviting rather than clinical and sterile. This provides customers with a reason to own a product or at the very least build a desire to purchase an item. The fourth reason is one where a good number of independent retailers can relate. Story telling allows retailers a chance to sell their 'onesies' or left over products at full price. One need not mark them down right away. By placing the products as part of a story, the items are given a new lease on life.

An independent retailer of home accessories, Drinkwater & Company understands the importance of story telling. Having a wide selection of products, they wanted to deliver a shopping experience unique to their store. They wanted their customers to have an enjoyable and memorable experience that they can take with them even when they leave the store. The photos next page show 'before' and 'after' photos that illustrate how products can be merchandised effectively by stories.

BEFORE

Breaking up the long aisle will allow for better customer flow as well as influence the eye to focus on one story at a time. The left photo shows three potential stories. The far left can be developed into a 'Shabby Chic' story, the middle section can be 'Modern Asian' while the right most have the beginnings of an 'Italian' story.

AFTER

Left: #1 Tuscan Afternoon
Below: #2 Asian Mod
Below Left: #3 Shabby Chic Influence

81

CASE STUDY: Drinkwater & Co

BEFORE
Categories merchandised in this section can be much improved by designating specific 'homes' for each story. In this case, the baby products do not encourage the sale of picnic bags, nor Italian oils.

AFTER (Below and next page)
Italian Oils are merchandised adjacent to Italian inspired dinnerware.

CASE STUDY: Drinkwater & Co

AFTER (Above): Picnic packs are displayed behind other picnic merchandise.
(Below): The baby group is merchandised on its own, separate from other stories.

83

CASE STUDY: Drinkwater & Company

CATEGORY PLACEMENT 'Before'

The categorization (refer to 'before' category plan next page) can be improved by creating tighter story groups. For example, Modern Asian dinnerware customers will hardly be tempted to add to their purchase, English or Italian Style merchandise.* When the goal is to increase incidence of multiple sales, it is just natural to display themes that share similar styles together.

Flowers are always a great bridge merchandise. Depending on colour and style, flowers will always find a home within differing stories. In this case, flowers were placed throughout the store based on where they may fit.

The 'After' category plan (next page) shows well grouped merchandise fitting within a story theme. Rustic Italian dinnerware combined with olive oils and earth tone accessories promote the sale of each group. Traditional and modern Asian merchandise create a cohesive theme while English dinnerware is housed within the Shabby Chic story. Basic items such as candles and feature items are given separate homes on the other side of the shop. Baby merchandise which do not fit within the home stories, is also given its own space.

Average sales per transaction increased from $24 to $42 *after the transformation*.

CASE STUDY: Drinkwater & Company

CATEGORY PLAN BEFORE

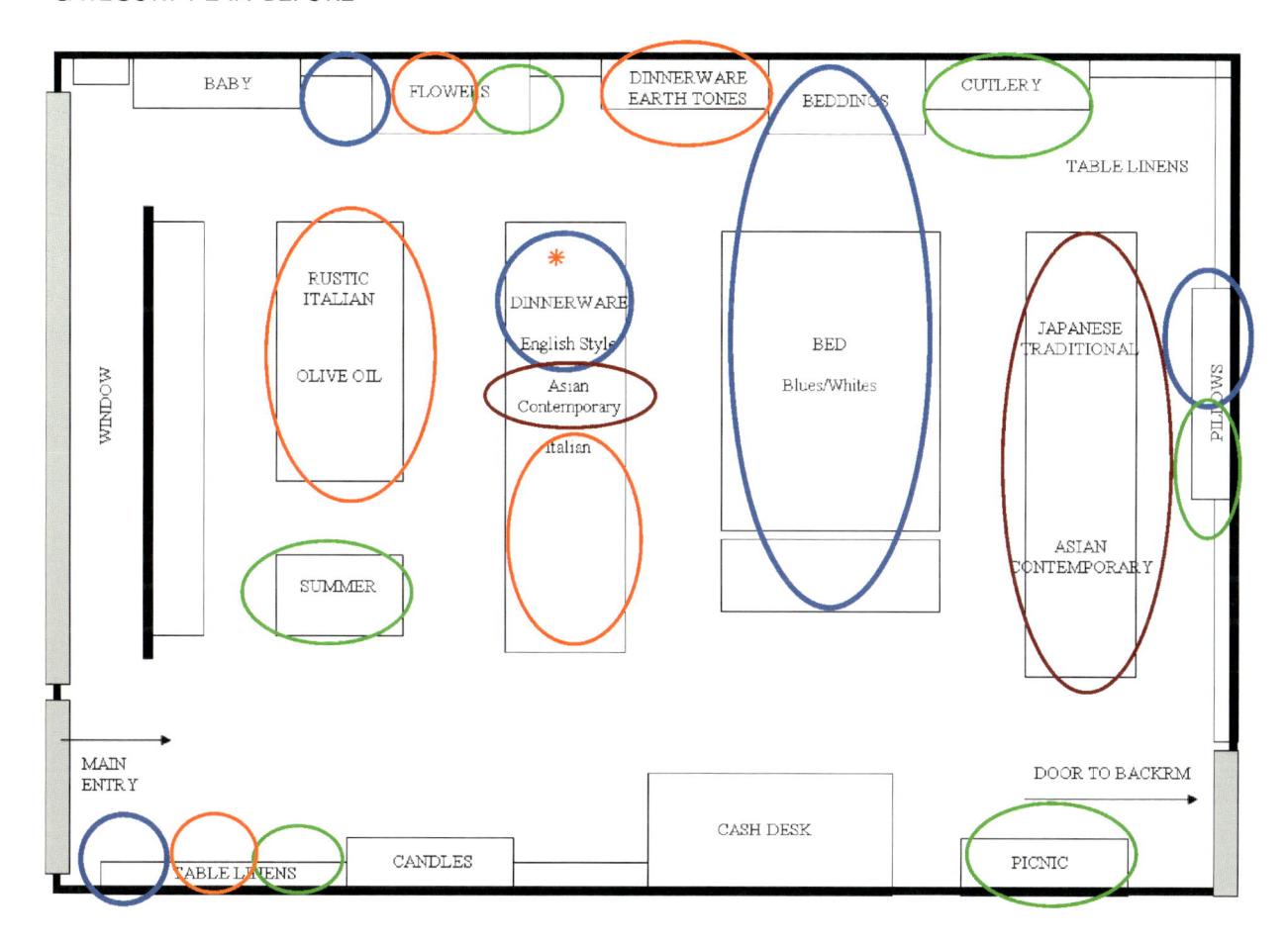

CATEGORY PLAN AFTER

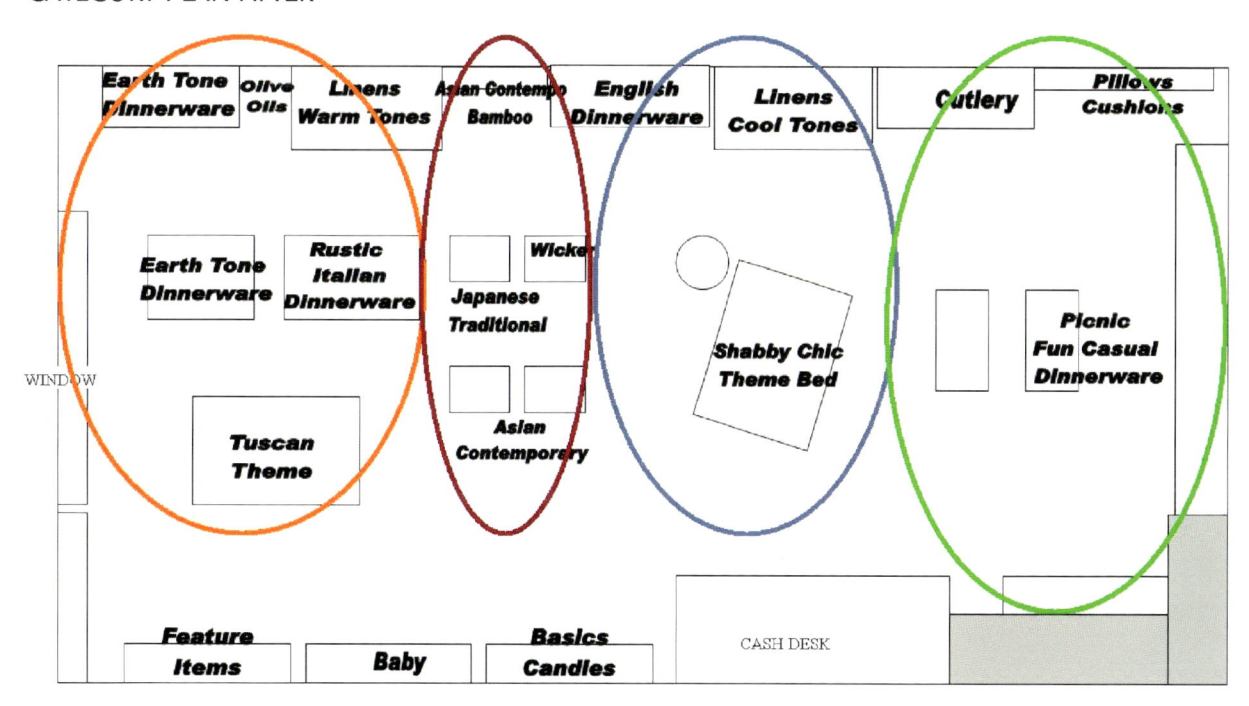

85

Themes and Lifestyle

Some retailers in the home accessories business opt to present product categories by themes or lifestyles. Tastes or styles range from traditional to modern; others may be purely cosmopolitan or ethnic.

Further sub-grouping may involve colour and fabrication. A fun, casual theme is built grouping accessories and products in vibrant colours made from materials such as glass or plastic. On the other hand, a classic, elegant story is conveyed by use of luxurious gold, silver and bronze colours in finely crafted metal or solid wood construction. Ethnic accents echo a proud cultural heritage such as African, Asian, European or Native Art.

CASE STUDY: Heavenly Outhouse, Cochrane Alberta

New shop owner Karrie Peace knew one thing for sure. She could improve sales and make the shop she purchased a favorite hang-out. It would have to change from the non too organized store it was. How to do this?

Karrie wanted to bring in large hand-made furniture from a local artisan. She had to incorporate these unique pieces with new merchandise she purchased, and old stock she inherited from the previous owner. Throughout the process, Karrie planned to reuse as much of the old existing fixtures as possible.

ADJACENCY PLAN & DISPLAY CASE STUDY 2: Heavenly Outhouse, Cochrane Alberta

We started by organizing categories. We considered where each new furniture piece would reside (E.G. barnwood vs. other wood finishes). After checking the designs of existing fixtures, we determined where they would be most effective, within a given category theme.

PHOTOS RIGHT & BOTTOM:

The first challenge was to find homes for differing wood furniture pieces by grouping like finishes together.

The next huge step was upon us; housing each product. A team of 4 merchandisers worked a total of 48 hours, segregating products into stories that each may fit in. Using florals as a 'bridge', a home was found for each item.

CASE STUDY: Heavenly Outhouse, Cochrane Alberta

The final layout was a merchandising success. According to Karrie, customers coming in are not only delighted, but she often hears people say "This is the most beautiful store I've ever seen!"

Logical Sequencing

Successful plays and stories contain an element that keeps the audience interested enough to go on. The same holds true in successful retailing. Let your plot unfold by Logical Sequencing. Lead customers from one product category to the other. This is the underlying factor which determines how long a potential customer stays in the store environment. The longer you are able to keep the customer browsing, the higher the likelihood of making a sale.

A men's clothing store, for example, may have a dominant clothing section, followed by leather goods, accessories or grooming products division. Similarly, a ladies' fashion store could follow the same flow of categories. Related products work together to build a more inclusive story for the customer.

The outline below shows how a retail store that caters to both genders can present their merchandise in an efficient and orderly manner. The product placement should allow for a smooth transition from one category to the next. The transition is not only smooth between categories; there is also a seamless crossing over between each.

This type of layout ensures that a sales team's active selling strategies are fully supported. It also allows for easy merchandise presentation options, since similar products are shown together. Building multiple selling opportunities becomes effortless not only within a category but also in crossing into the next group.

Preferences and Priorities

Joseph Weishar, author of Design for Effective Selling Space, maintains "the sequence of selection by the customer must be mirrored in the sequence of product presentation." He reminds us that customers not only have pre-set shopping preferences, but these preferences vary. Outside factors, such as seasonality, often affect what we like at a certain time.

A good way to appreciate preference shopping is to look more closely at typical purse buying. Women who purchase prestige designer handbags have an unmistakable shopping priority. They are part of a target market that makes buying decisions for reasons of prestige, social standing, peer acceptance and status. Product priority lies in the designer name.

A high-end department store or a duty free store will often present an exclusive shop-within-a-shop layout. Here, designer brands and lifestyle take centre stage. These areas grab shoppers' interest at the entrance or on a feature wall.

Alternatively, let's look at another group of women; shoppers who give lower priority to brands and higher priority to finding the right price. In this case, brand is not the main concern. Handbags with gengeneric or unrecognizable brand names are best displayed by style. You'll find these merchandise stories revolve around styles for casual, formal, business, sports, or travel wear, rather than by designer name.

Not all products are displayed with customers' ease of shopping in mind. Some are merchandised depending on suppliers' preferences. There is a growing number of suppliers who will carry the cost of fixturing plus labour. This expenditure is a way for them to influence how their own products are presented.

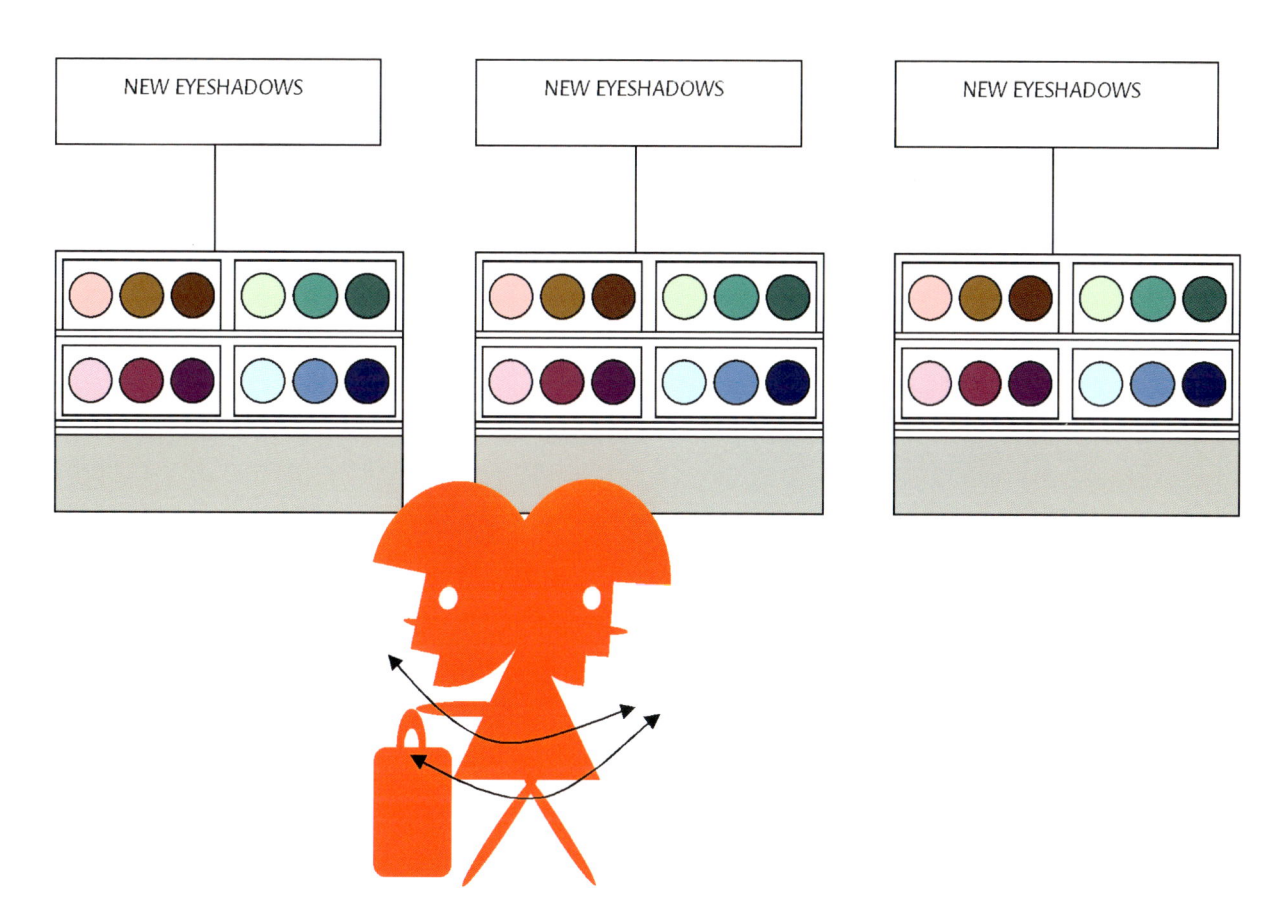

Exceptions To The Rule

Any woman who uses cosmetics will tell you stores present them by brand. I have to ask: does this make sense? As a regular cosmetic shopper, wouldn't it be easier if we could approach one section that has all the latest colours of eye shadows displayed together? This way, we wouldn't have to stop at all 16 brand displays to see recent colour trends.

True, but suppliers do not want cosmetic shoppers to 'one-stop' shop. Maybe, just maybe, the game plan of cosmetics suppliers is to reinforce brand loyalty. Aha! Their insistence on displaying products by brand could make sense. If you have already shopped for ABC eye shadow, you'll find ABC blush and lipstick just a few inches away.

Anyone whose gone fragrance shopping can relate to another of my pet peeves. I love the soothing scent of lavender. However, how do I begin a quest for finding lavender-scented fragrances without having to sniff at least twenty other aroma-filled bottles?
I believe fragrances and essential oils should be displayed according to scent. I can't help but wonder why we are so accepting of the current mixed situation. Why do so few people complain about how time consuming fragrance shopping is currently?

An alternate display strategy would be to separate floral from citrus scents. Division by aroma makes complete sense (pardon the pun) to someone like me, who does not relish the thought of having to go on a bottle sniffing marathon.

In fact Someone must be listening to my prayers. Recently, I drove to Seattle for a day trip, and made a discovery that convinced me I was in shopping heaven. Nordstrom's has fragrances displayed according to scent! They use open shelving units, making bottles easily accessible, and allow customers to test fragrances happily, without fear of being serviced by an eager sales associate, before they are ready to make a commitment. Hallelujah!

Learning From Children

Toy stores and book stores are among everyone's favourite places to shop. The Adjacency Plan in many of these has been raised to an art.

Notice how easy it is to shop when products are already grouped by end use? All baby products are in one section, adjacent to the toddlers, which are divided into familiar characters such as Caillou, Dora, Blues Clues, etc. How fortunate for busy moms, and aunts like me.

Shopping for my niece and nephew is a breeze as there are clear delineations between boys' and girls' sections. Category distinction does not stop at gender. Toys aimed for each are further sub-categorized by groups. Boys' sections feature action figures by character, or sports supplies, like basketballs, baseballs, and soccer balls. In the girls' corner, toys are categorized by their preferred pastimes; Princess Dolls, Barbies and Bratz, for example.

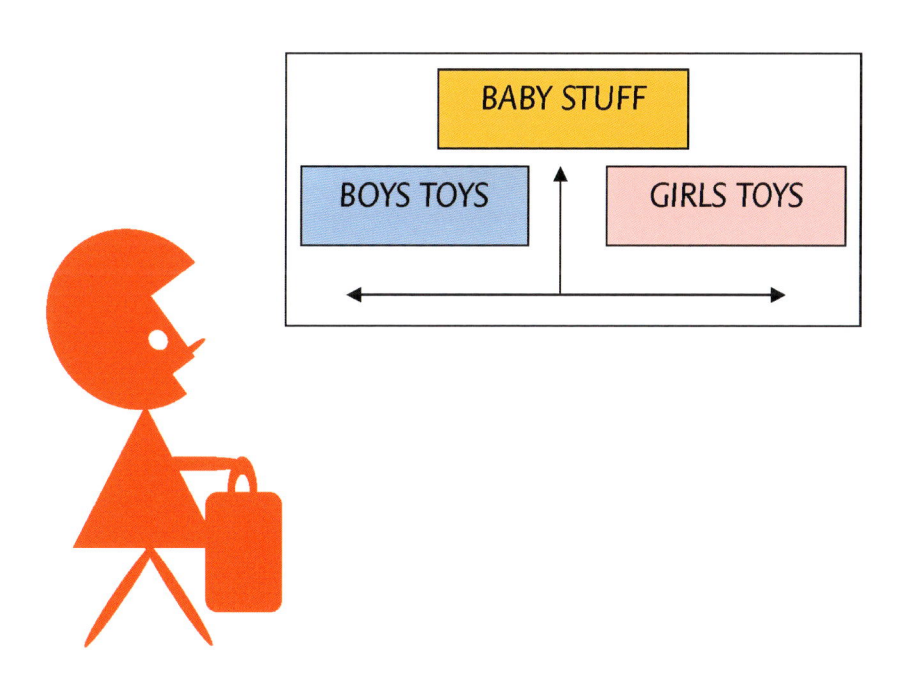

Bookstores tend to group by genre, age group and, when it comes to children, reading level. These kinds of separations make it easy to find what you are looking for. Imagine the utter chaos of not having a sensible classification system for an inventory of a thousand books.

Product Classification

It is an open secret that visual merchandising strategies vary according to gender predispositions. When shopping for shoes, the first thing I look for is style. Brand is secondary as long as I love the look and fit (maybe). Besides, sizes vary from one brand to the other, including shoe widths.

My husband, on the other hand, tends to go back to the same store which carries the brand he likes. He not only has far fewer pairs than I do – we are looking at a 25:1 ratio! - but he surmises he's already found the one brand he needs. Their fit is perfect. Why waste time and try a "hundred" more pairs? My husband is a dream customer; one that is not only loyal to one store, but also loyal to one brand. Come on guys, where's the fun in that?!

A typical women's shoe store displays merchandise by style, under various footwear classifications, like high heels or career styles. A standard men's shoe store, on the contrary, will merchandise by brand name because it makes choosing easier for their target customers.

Basics, Seasonals and Impulse Buys

What about stores carrying products that can be classified as basics, seasonals or impulse buys?

Basics are perennial must-have items that customers seek out time and again. Place them towards the back Power Wall. This ensures other merchandise gets double exposure: as customers walk to the back for that pair of basic blue jeans, and then returning to the front for the cash and wrap.

Seasonals typically have a shorter shelf life. Display these items upfront or place them where there is high traffic. Near a Story Wall, Power Wall, intersection, or 'Strike Zone' is a good spot for seasonals. Close by the cash desk is also suitable, as customers waiting in line will get to view the product.

Impulse items, on the other hand, are great anywhere they can complement a particular product. For example, dress socks coordinated with a smart 2-piece outfit display may also be visible by the cash desk, and of course, along the socks wall. Think about chip clips in the chip aisle; they can be double displayed again on the aisle stocking kitchen gadgets. You get the idea.

ADJACENCY PLAN & DISPLAY CASE STUDY 3: Community Natural Foods

With a strong niche market, Community Natural Health Foods in Calgary created a health section separate from groceries. With strong sales from supplements and natural body care, an expansion was called for. The original category plan below can be improved by analyzing destination points. This will allow the shop to maximize selling opportunities and lessen challenged areas.

In the original plan below, gifts and skincare are located to the back of the main entry point. This peripheral category could better perform if the core basic essentials is located here instead. This will ensure visits to gifts and other non-essentials as customers walk towards and out of the basics section.

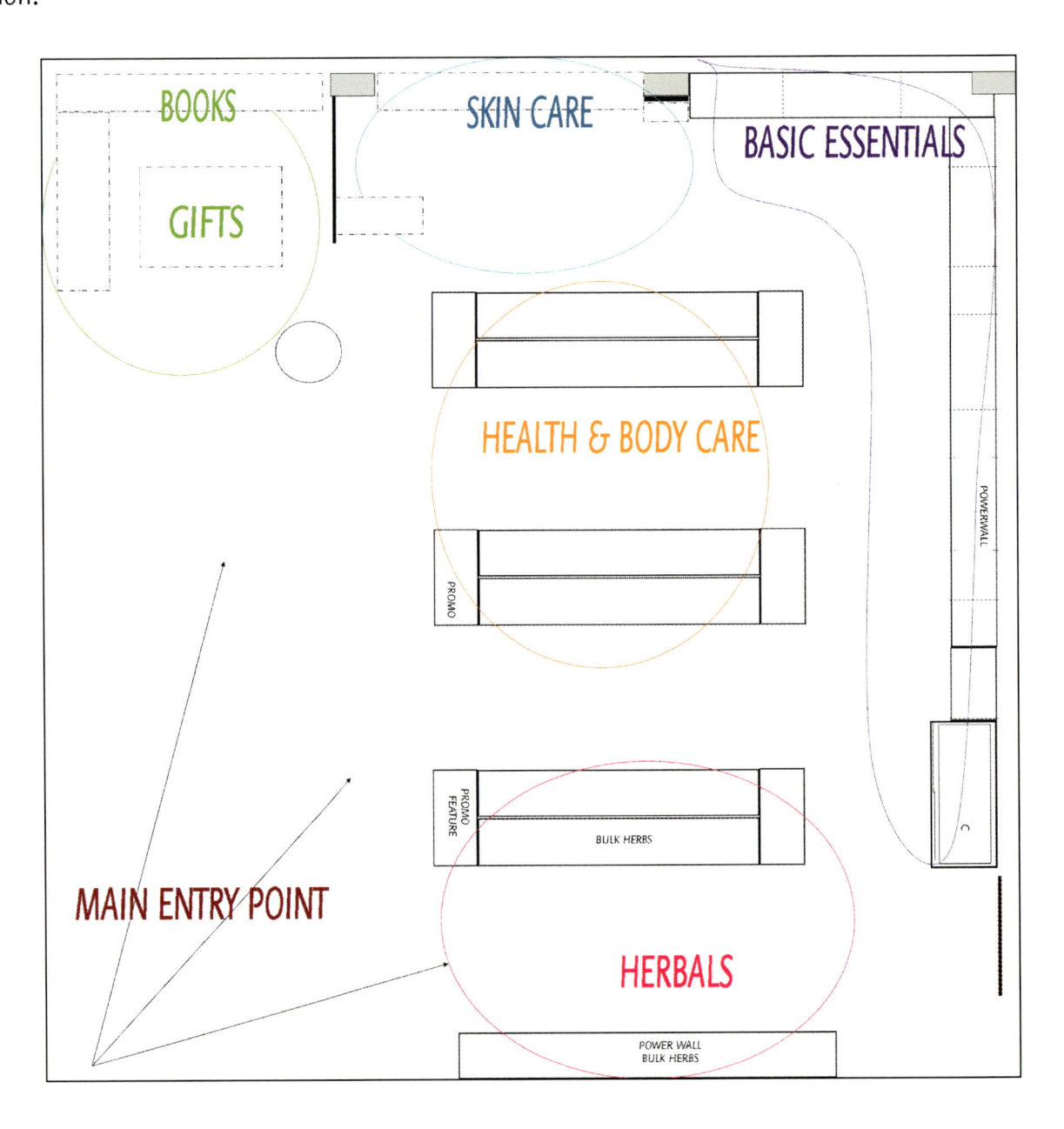

CASE STUDY: Community Natural Foods

The new layout shows two entry points with feature areas immediately greeting these entrances. The back most section in this case becomes the top right corner where basic essentials are housed. Customers shopping for these basics will be exposed to non-essential peripheral merchandise as they walk towards the essentials and also on their way out of the selling space.

"After seeing Natalie's presentation at the Canadian Health Foods Association West Show, I was excited at the idea of working with someone as energetic and insightful about retail merchandising as she is. In choosing to work with Natalie, I was not disappointed: her expertise greatly helped us at an important stage of our store renovations."

Kim Ryrie, HABC Category Manager, Community Foods Ltd.

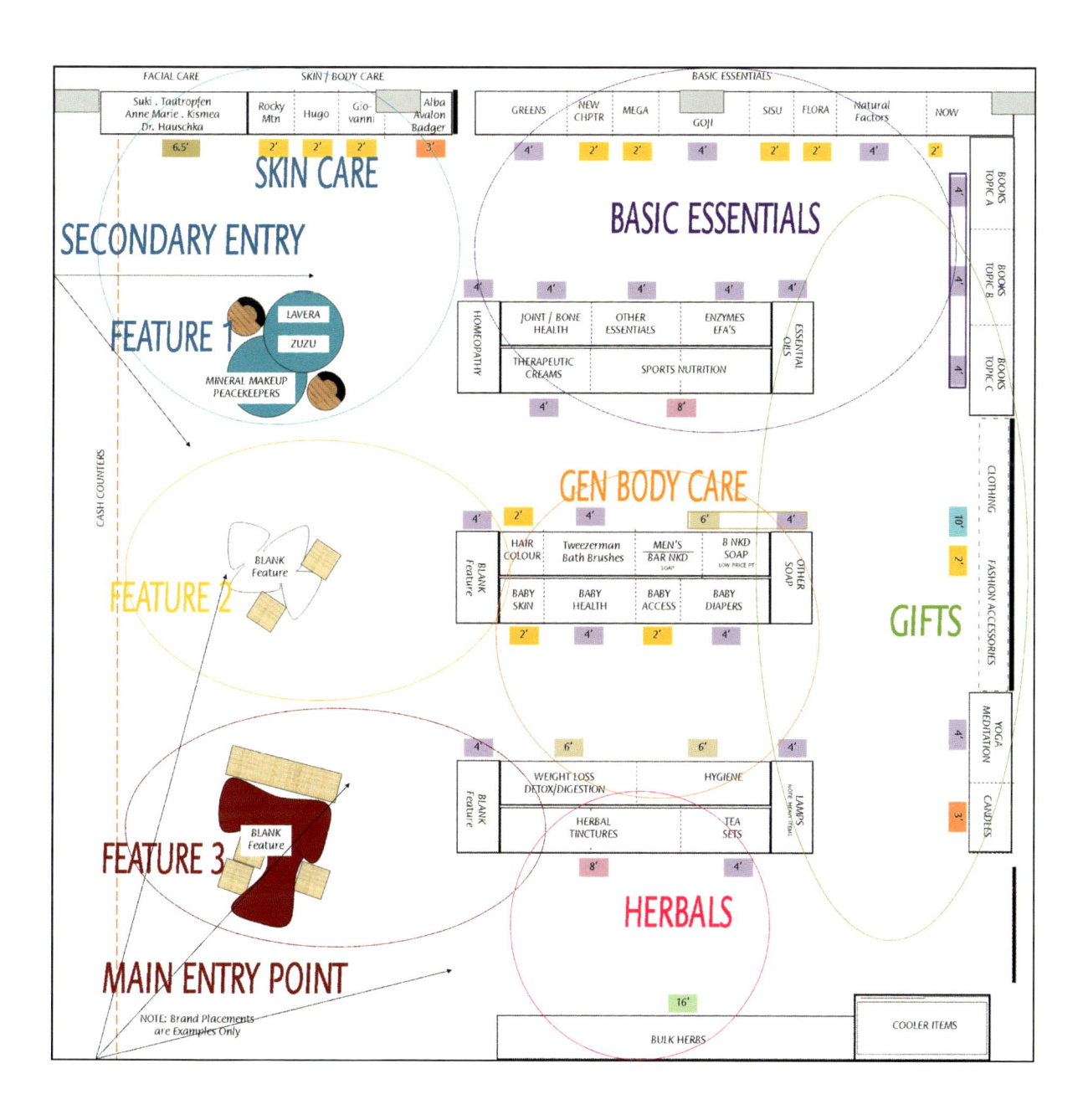

ADJACENCY PLAN & DISPLAY CASE STUDY 4: Barron Heating

An inviting space welcomes all customers visiting Barron Heating in Mt. Vernon, Washington. Living room spaces, kitchen and dining displays all provide one with a warm and cozy place to shop. While living room fireplaces may be beautiful to look at, backroom furnaces are hardly romantic. In the original category plan, furnaces were placed in a separate area with its own entrance. Urban fireplaces and stoves were then located in the main showroom. Integrating these two creates a challenge. However it is vital that they be combined since both are integral to home heating solutions. Regardless of target market, both trade and the public now have a chance to view all.

ORIGINAL CATEGORY PLAN
While the intention of the small main entrance is to drive customers to both the heating section and the 'spa & backyards' shop on the other side, it instead drives customers directly into furnaces. It is only when customers turn left that they see displays of fireplaces. Even if the original entrance is used, separate entrances mean customers do not necessarily see all home heating solutions presented. From the main entrance, urban fireplaces first greet customers while wood stoves are all displayed to the back of the showroom. Due to narrow aisles and a highly sectionalized space, customers may altogether miss this section.

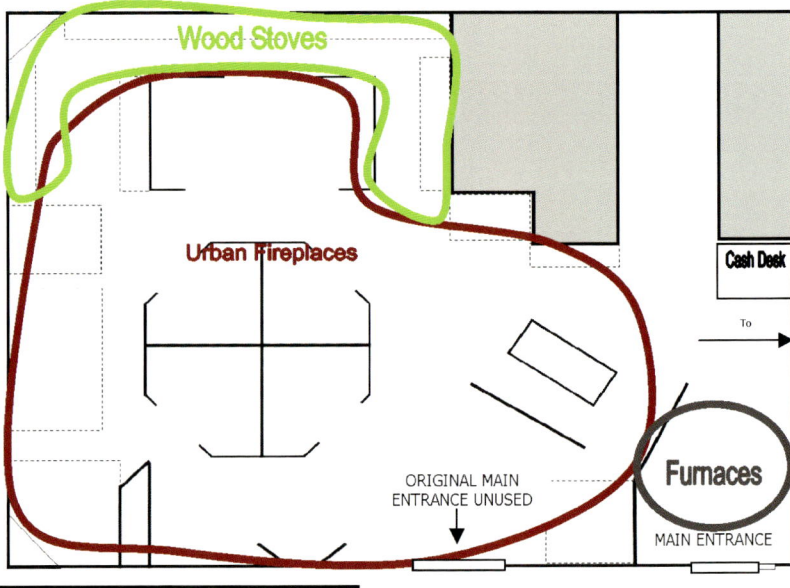

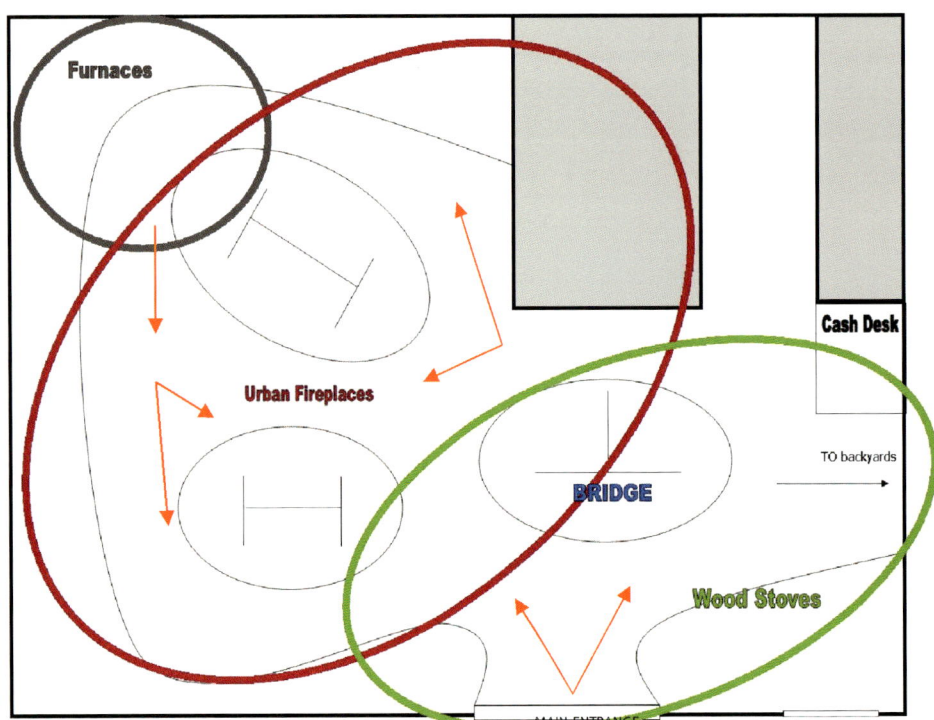

REVISED CATEGORY PLAN
With a racetrack layout angled directly from the main entrance, customers are now flanked on both sides with wood stoves and urban fireplace vignettes. The welcoming editorial spaces invites customers to walk further into the racetrack layout. As they round the track, furnaces are showcased at the back, ensuring that customers do not miss this vital home heating solution section.

"Natalie has a keen sense of the retail business and what it takes to make the sale. She provides a laser focus on creating an effective showroom layout. She has benefited our company through increased sales but also in teaching our staff to look at our showroom through the eyes of our customers."
John Barron, Owner, Barron Heating & Air Conditioning

ADJACENCY PLAN & DISPLAY CASE STUDY 5: Sample The UPS Stores®

The UPS Stores® sell convenience, fast and secure delivery of parcels and ease of doing business. While one of their core product is package delivery, The UPS Store® customers rely on service convenience. For both small business operators and the public, quick and reliable printing services as well as postal boxes are as vital as shipping. Other conveniences such as access to computers, photocopying and availability of packaging supplies and other office supplies are what their customers expect to find.

Ensuring that all peripheral offerings flank customers as they enter the selling space can enhance customer experience. This also encourages impulse sales and suggestive selling as customers walk toward the service counter and as they leave the shop.

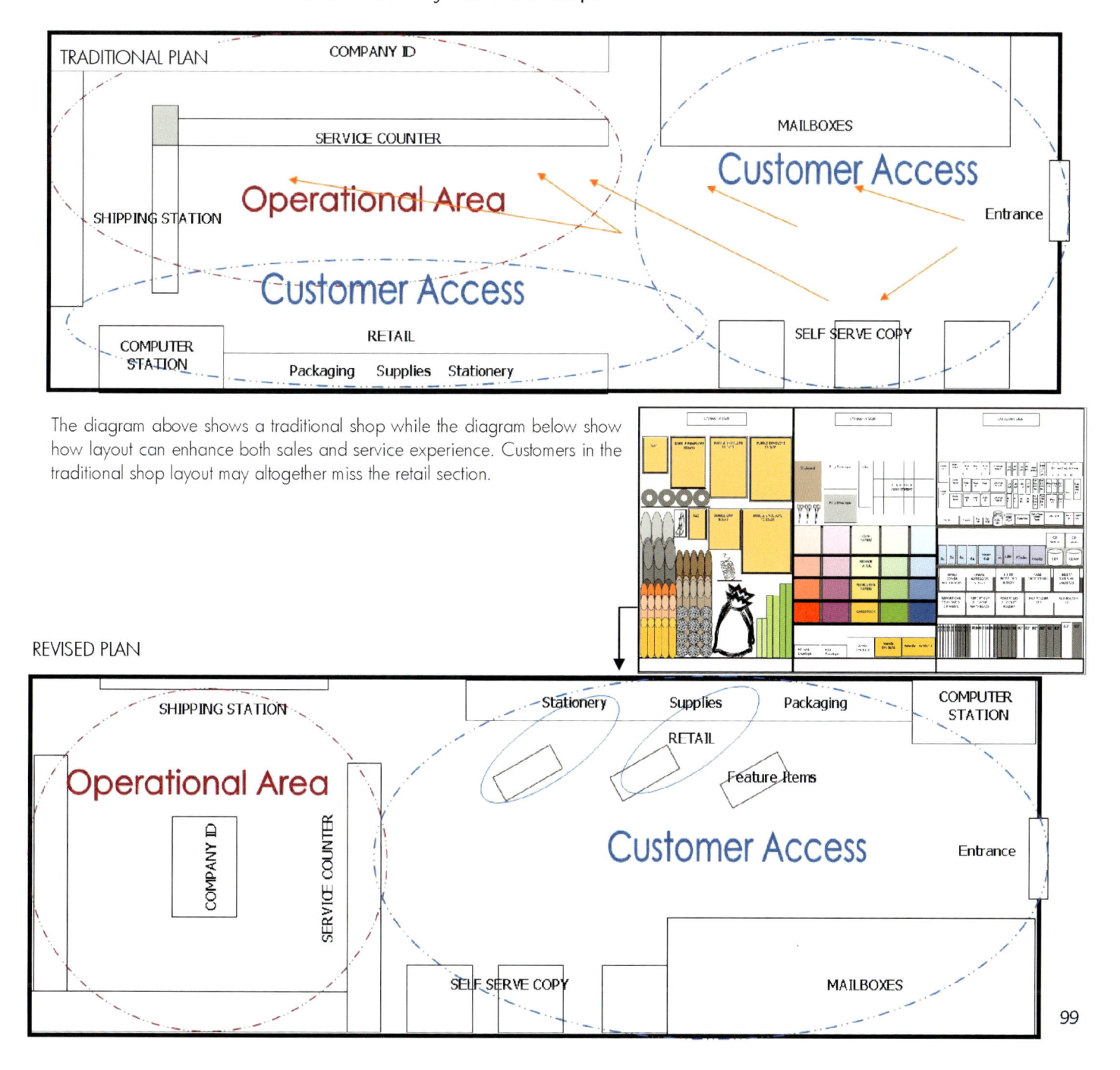

The diagram above shows a traditional shop while the diagram below show how layout can enhance both sales and service experience. Customers in the traditional shop layout may altogether miss the retail section.

ADJACENCY PLAN & DISPLAY CASE STUDY 6: Color O Living

As a specialty home store, Color O Living had to work with a very wide range of merchandise in varying price points. Finding the right place for each group was a challenge. Only 4 major stories were recommended for the store size. Grouping different items into tight clustered themes was the only recourse. Irrationality of Combinations, here we come!

In the end, we were able to establish three distinct stories. Casual Fun covers all the brightly coloured and popularly priced merchandise. Natural Earth includes merchandise that falls into this colour group. Classic Elegance embraces the gold, silver and copper colours. A middle 'bridge' area was created to feature new merchandise from either theme.

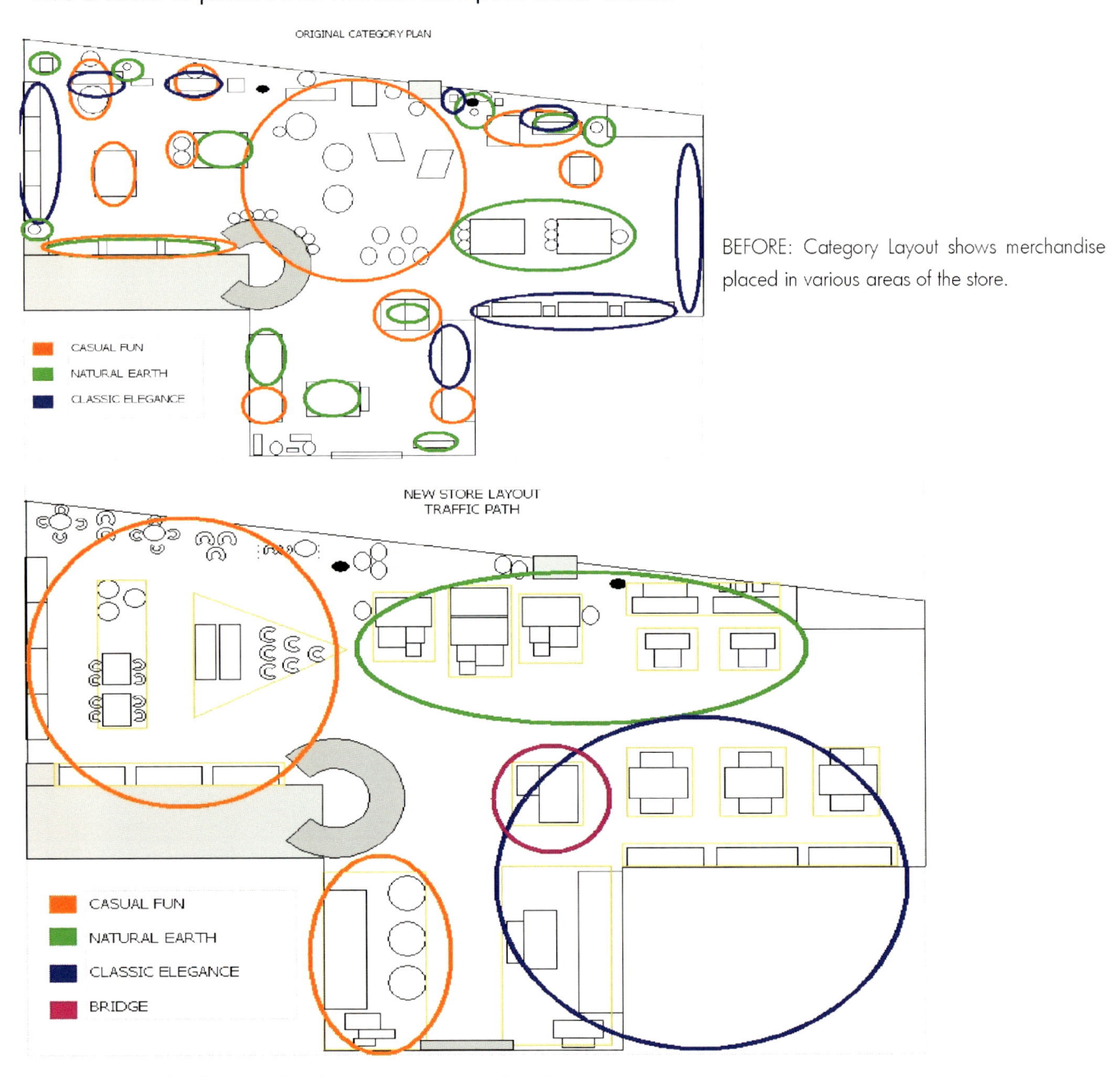

BEFORE: Category Layout shows merchandise placed in various areas of the store.

AFTER: A streamlined approach with each story in its own 'home'.

100

Though several presentation strategies were introduced, a dominant approach creates a sense of movement or 'Rhythm' in each display. Products become more inviting to touch. The photo below shows a horizontal or flat presentation. The left photo shows how introducing rhythm makes merchandise more appealing.

The new set-up below draws the eye in and out of the display, as well as up and down. This creates interest and draws eyes to the display.

101

Ensuring congruence not only in grouping but also price point is vital if you want to provide a smooth shopping experience. The left photo below shows very affordably priced chairs (Casual Fun) adjacent to higher priced hand made pieces (Classic Elegance). The improved set-up on the right promotes only one story at a time - in this case, Casual Fun.

Implementing these strategies is not only fun and interesting, but the end results make shopping a more pleasurable experience. No comment sums this up better than something David Lui, then President of Thomson and Fenn Trading, has said.

"Customers respond positively to the atmosphere and many are come in just to see what new displays we have." For Color O Living, proper Category Adjacency was part of the solution that helped beat the post holiday blues!

Strategic Product Placement

Strategic product placement works to emphasize the need to ensure each item suggestively sells adjacent merchandise as well. Successful stores will maximize multiple selling opportunities. Adjacent product placement is paramount to increased sales per transaction.

When you attract customers into a specific section of the store, capitalize on the opportunity to present merchandise in an easy to understand sequence. Apply the following visual merchandising tactics:

- Create displays that beg to be touched and have merchandise taken home to its rightful owner
- Design enjoyable encounters. If the shopping experience in your store is fun and stress free, chances are customers will come back for more happy endings

I found the best way to teach people how to put what products where, is to share some successful changes. Join me as we work through how stores I've worked with arrive at decisions on product categories and product stories.

STORE TRANSFORMATION 1: LALA HOME DECOR (HOME DÉCOR)

Merchandising Strategies within a category, sub-category and shelving unit.

What exactly is a store transformation and what does it do? For Kristina Egyed of Lala Décor, it meant turning her store inside out. The changes she made achieved an average of 20% increase in sales per transaction, and a 16% increase in units per transaction. Those enhanced sales stayed consistent month after month.

In the heart of Deep Cove, North Vancouver, B.C., an eclectic home décor store called LaLa was ready for a change. A change in market demographics calls for a merchandise revamp. It was time for a new name, a new look, and a new store.

First, the current layout was analyzed. How do people walk and shop the store? Are they penetrating all the way back or are they boomeranging? This analysis was followed by a close look at fixture placement. As with most owners, a universal cry of "I don't have enough room" was plain. Hence, spatial intensity was reviewed and a new strategy implemented.

Next, Kristina worked to ensure that each customer bought more than one item. This meant organizing categories so that each section was flanked by a complementary category. For example, the previous set-up had serene bath products next to funky gifts, with dinnerware adjacent to rugs. In the new arrangement, aromatic bath products were placed along with Asian decorative accessories to create a dynamic serene section. This promoted each category while creating a more positive impact as shoppers entered. The grouping encouraged multiple sales per transaction. To capitalize on rug sales, they were grouped with furniture, mirrors and coordinating accessories. The result was a collection that promoted the sale of each item in it.

STORE TRANSFORMATION 1: LALA HOME DÉCOR

Cross merchandising between categories not only supports purchasing from each section, but also builds a smooth flow from one area to the next. Dinnerware and linens have obvious multiple selling potential. Items were used from each category to create focal points. This result has linens selling in sets, as well as complimenting sales of related dinnerware.

To top everything off, one of Kristina's great selling allies today is her effective signage. Organizing the store by creating boutiques within the shop makes shopping fun and easy. Supplementing this technique with category and point of purchase signage further advances an impression of entertainment and fun. Best of all, well-organized, professional signage promotes retail image and identity.

The original layout failed to propel people deep into the store. Tight fixture placements made access difficult. Tall fixtures also blocked views of the rest of the shop. The resulting environment missed opportunities to influence eye movement and achieve full penetration. Additionally, categories were not grouped tightly enough. Customers found the same category items in different parts of the store. In the above diagram, each category is circled in a specific colour to depict before and after locations.

STORE TRANSFORMATION 1: LALA HOME DÉCOR

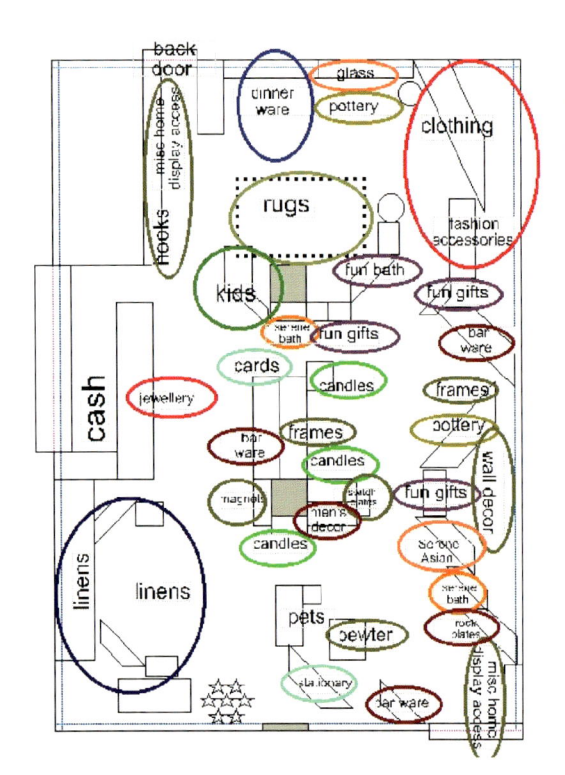

BEFORE: Each colour represents a category. While customers may find appealing individual merchandise, it is hard to shop when merchandise that share the same category are located in various places.

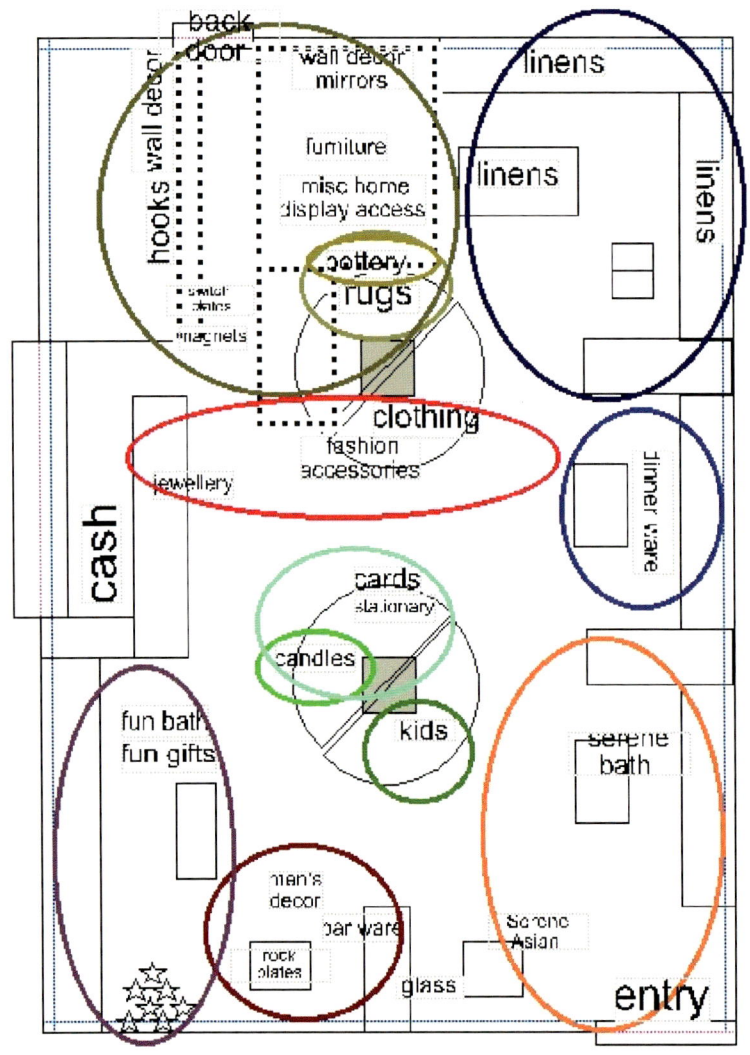

AFTER: Creating a flow that invited customers to further shop the selling space means creating adjacency benefits. For example, kitchen and bath; linens between kitchen and home accessories; and fun gifts with bar ware.

106

STORE TRANSFORMATION 1: LALA HOME DECOR

The new layout creates an easier flow from the entrance all the way to the back. The Racetrack layout provides an opportunity to invent mini shops within Lala. We designed small 'atmospheres' and they work together to deliver a much fuller shopping experience. The improved category layout also ensures adjacent sections complement each other. Strike Zones are utilized to introduce new categories. Displays are arranged that work in relation to each other. For example, locating the kids section across from the bath and kitchen section allows mothers a watchful eye on their children while they play around the area.

Examine the new layout and category adjacencies carefully and you'll find it is easy to comprehend the reasoning behind relocation. Clothing was once at the back of the store flanked by pottery, glass and fun gifts. The enhanced layout places clothing close to jewelry and fashion accessories, which encourages multiple sales. Fun gifts are located close to bar ware and men's gifts. Large furniture items are placed at the back of the store along with rugs, mirrors and other home accessories.

Another advantage of the new layout is that it allows staff to move one section in a different location more simply, as needed. For example, if there is a shipment of new furniture to promote, staff at LaLa Home Decor can move it up close to the windows, fitting it in along with mirrors and other home accessories. A workable layout encourages the movement of merchandise around the store, thereby giving the perception of 'always something new.'

STORE TRANSFORMATION 2: CLOSE TO YOU LINGERIE
(CLOTHING LINGERIE)

Beckoning, Seducing, Selling
The Secret to A Small Town Store's Success

Parksville, B.C. is not often at the top of the list when we think of red-hot retailing towns, famous for exceptional returns. Sandy Herle, owner of Close To You Lingerie, is proof that the sleepy reputation of this small town on the eastern shores of Vancouver Island can be changed. She not only transformed her store into a sales power house, but Sandy successfully expanded into a new location, adding a full clothing line.

When we first made contact at the beginning of the holiday season, I empathized with her need for better store organization. The seasonal merchandise had just arrived, and the small store was bursting at the seams. For Sandy, Close To You had lost its very essence; romance and seduction.

I come across many retailers like Sandy whose original intention is to have fun delivering great service while at the same time providing a unique shopping atmosphere. Somewhere along the line, store operations, inventory planning and management take up such a bulk of time that the initial romance is drained slowly away.

To get back to those inspiring original roots, ask yourself why customers shop your store. What is it that differentiates you from chain stores or big box retailers? What do customers want out of your product?

In Sandy's case, it was romance, seduction, comfort, the right fit and knowledgeable staff. From this straight forward answer we re-designed store layout and came up with a workable Category Adjacency plan.

STORE TRANSFORMATION 2: CLOSE TO YOU LINGERIE

A seasonal section greets customers as they walk in. With the cold, windy Parksville weather, shoppers were straight away seduced by thick huggable robes merchandised with comfy flannels. Once inside, the snuggables gave way to soft, flowy romantic robes and lingerie, perfect for a night spent in front of the fireplace with a glass of wine. Next, customers are treated to garments designed with one thing in mind...seduction. Towards the back of the store, a Power Wall is lined with the basics. It's a spot where service experts can linger, ready to fit customers.

Fast forward to a year later. According to Sandy, "With the improved divisions and groupings, clients spend more time in the store exploring and discovering. They are able to go to the area of their wants, and everything is tied together with purpose and direction. We see nothing but great things happening here." Sandy concludes, "Our overall October sales went up 83%! For starters, bra sales were up 26 %. Even panty sales went up 19%."

BEFORE

AFTER

LAST WORDS

Make Shopping Easy!

Is your store an Olympic Venue?

Do customers have to jump through hoops, kneel, squat, reach and extend?

Shopping should be easy. In a world where Baby Boomers are in their 40s, 50s and 60s, physical requirements have changed. I count myself as part of the Boomers; the tail end of the group, of course! I find myself pushing an item a few inches away just to be able to read the label. When did lighting levels change? When did crouching down to look for my size become a symphony of grunts, cracks and groans? Have stores changed the shelving unit levels and put them closer to the ground? What's with aisles: Did I become wider and that's why I find it hard to navigate in between? Maybe stores narrowed their aisles. That's it!

RIGHT: Please don't make aisles narrower than they already are.

LEFT: Please, oh please, I beg you, do not make me crouch and kneel down to reach for the small items. I may not be able to get back up!

110

RIGHT: Can someone please turn the lights up?

Breathe in, stretch. Stretch again and breathe out. Now, forward fold. Good. A warm-up routine is almost necessary before any serious shopping. I marvel at stores who make it harder for me to buy. Avoid making it difficult for a shopper to find an item. Considering that purchasing decisions are mostly made in-store, retailers must give careful thought to how they present merchandise. Most people will pick items within eye and waist levels. The standard for merchandising products is for the small items to be within eye to arm level, medium items waist level and large items below this but at least a foot off the floor.

When housing one product type, this theory will probably result with large items being left unsold. A better ideas is to put all 3 sizes in one shelf uniformly throughout the entire unit. That way, shoppers have the easy option of picking the size they want. For clothing, try placing large shirts on the top shelf and small ones on the bottom, instead of the other way around? This makes sense, since large-sized shoppers will find it harder to crouch than smaller-sized ones? Think about the customer. Shop your store and see where you can make it easier for them.

Natalie Tan provides clients with the tools to excel in their business. Over 25 years in specialty retailing and shopping centre management has provided Natalie with the expertise to offer innovative strategies to malls, retail shops and airport operators in maximizing their revenue. Natalie currently teaches Merchandising and Display Strategies at the British Columbia Institute of Technology School of Business. She served as a member of Retail BC's Board of Directors and is currently serving on the British Columbia Shopping Centres Association's board. Visit the Retail Excellence website at www.retailexcellence.com.